Godless Satanism Doctrine

LCFNS
Lucifer Nostra Salus

SS-Ecclesia Luciferi 2024

Contents

„For the devil's word is alive and has sinful power, sharper than the nails of golgoth, it penetrates deep, separates flesh from spirit, bone from soul, recognises the instincts and intentions of the unconscious. There is no being hidden from its truth".

Biblia Satanae, Etd. 4.12

Introduction

The Godless Gospel of Ecclesia Luciferi

To Live Deliciously

The power of religion is based almost exclusively on speculation and emotion, the belief in the reward of an eternal life, free of all suffering and pain, which will come after death, and the fear of death or eternal torture in hell. Also important is the inculcated sense of guilt, the constant conviction that one has done something wrong, or has already inherited an evil, corrupted nature and is therefore guilty of something, completely unspecified but evil, from birth. To this must also be added the message that man is weak and worthless and unable to save himself without an imaginary deity who is the only one able to save man from himself, from his nature.

This brief characterisation roughly describes every theistic faith, and in particular is a brief summary of the message of the Christian gospel.

The theistic Christian gospel can thus be characterised in a fairly concise way.

And can it be conveyed in an equally concise way what the godless gospel of Ecclesia Luciferi teaches?

The doctrine of Ecclesia Luciferi was created for the benefit of some, for those who dare to abandon faith, hope and love for delusion and who fearlessly confront the unforgiving, morally indifferent, brutal truth about the true nature of things.

So that the Satanist, having rejected belief in imaginary gods, will believe in the divinity of the reason of the human animal, and in the abundant, godless life before death, and that, knowing it to be the inevitable end, he will have eternal peace after death, united forever with the power of the Infinite, the only godless reality that exists.

Or even more succinctly:

That man may so love the godless world that he may reject the belief in delusion which takes away the power of the divinity of human reason, and that he may not become a slave to the fear of hell, but have a godless life abundant before eternity in the peace of death.

Satanic Restoration

Profession of Disbelief

Accepting Satanism according to the Ecclesia Luciferi means returning the person to a state of original godlessness. Primordial godlessness is the natural state of every newborn person. No child will believe in any made-up god on its own until belief in theistic delusions is transferred to it by parents or religious teachers. A person who deeply understands the essence of the evil of theistic error and expresses the will to actively oppose it becomes an adversary of the theistic god in the image of Satan, becomes a Satanist. In such a person there is a godless restoration. The state of original godlessness is not yet Satanism, it is atheism. Only the recognition of the essence of the theistic god and the will to oppose it leads to Satanism. Since the greatest crime according to theism is unbelief, the Satanist must rid himself completely of any belief in theistic delusions. In doing so, the Satanist commits a mortal sin.

The natural indifference and lack of religious morality of the natural world is seen by theists as the fall of nature into sin due to Satan's rebellion. Therefore, living until death in a state of natural sin, devoid of theistic morality is proper to the Satanist.

The declaration of Satanic Restoration according to Ecclesia Luciferi is an understanding and acceptance of the claims of godless Satanism:

There is no god but Satan, whose image arises and visualises itself in my own mind, every day more and more, who is the symbol of the eternal, unchanging and indifferent laws of fallen nature, who symbolises mortal life in flesh and blood and eternal death that gives eternal peace. There are no messiahs and prophets above myself, whose intelligence leads me to recognise the true nature of things. There are no gods. There is nothing there!

By rejecting all theistic beliefs the Satanist becomes a theistic apostate. A self-willed return to original godlessness - Satanic Restoration means sinning against the Holy Spirit. Satanic apostasy is therefore an unforgivable act in the light of theistic theologies. The Satanist, through the act of apostasy, therefore accepts death as the final end of the only life in flesh and blood. Satanic restoration means the death of faith in the hereafter and the hope of the unfounded promise of life after life.

The Satanist by his attitude, behaviour, words and intelligence should even vaguely provoke those around him to take an interest in the anti-theistic philosophy of the mystery of godlessness, which to those who understand and accept it gives the power to live abundantly here and now, in flesh and blood, without fear of death

and a vengeful god in the hereafter. Living abundantly, full of satanic pride, without fear or guilt and in accordance with the eternal laws of nature can be very attractive and rewarding. Fear is an integral part of any theistic religion. It is one of the powers of theism that drives so many followers to it. The Satanism of Ecclesia Luciferi is devoid of fear.

After these introductory words, it is necessary to begin by explaining what Satanism is and who Satan is.

Traditional Satanism

Martin John-Satan presiding at the Infernal Council 1824

The term Satanism derives from the concept of Satan, who is a figure originating from the Yahwist tradition.

In the article: **"The Meaning and Function of Satan in the Hebrew Bible** (Old Testament) its author **Leonce F. Rambau** writes about the origin of the term Satan this way:

"In the first two chapters of the Book of Job, we encounter a heavenly figure, identified as the Satan (hassatan) who is described as one of "the sons of God."

The noun Satan is derived from the verb Sãtan, with the Semitic root śtn. The noun occurs 27 times in the Hebrew Bible (Old Testament), while the verb Sãtan occurs 6 times. Other related forms are śitna, śatam, and mastema, which are well attested in the Hebrew Bible.

The meaning of the verb satan is variously rendered as "to accuse," "to slander," or "to be an adversary." Sãtan is a pure Semitic word in early use among the Israelites.

Satan in the Old Testament appears in the following verses: Numbers 22:22, 32; Zachariah 3:1; Job 1–2; and 1 Chronicles 21:1

A careful analysis of the verses in which the figure of Satan appears shows his evolution in the Old Testament. According to the author of the article, first there is the appearance and development of the "heavenly" Satan in the four texts in which he appears, and the use of this name first describes his divine function, but slowly this function became more and more detached from God, and in the last text, i.e., 1 Chronicles 21:1, this character acts independently.

Rabbinical literature also speaks interestingly about Satan. **Edward Langton**, in his book **Essentials of Demonology**, quotes the following passages from the Talmud on this subject:

"In T.B. Baba Bathra (16a) Satan is identified with the Yetzer ha Ra, 'evil impulse' in man. This appears to be a rationalistic attempt to account for Satan as a personification of the evil inclination in man. As a rule, the Talmud not only distinguishes between a personal Satan without, and an evil inclination within, man, but also expressly ascribes to God the creation of the Yetzer ha Ra in man in the condition in which he was before the fall. In T.B. Berachoth (61a) it is argued that the occurrence of the two yodhs (yy) in the word Wayyicer ('and he formed', Genesis 27) indicates the existence of two impulses in man—the Yetzer Tobh and the Yetzer ha Ra."
(Compare with the concept of Zaorstrian dualism, which I write about in one of the next chapters of this book.)

In T.B. Yoma (69b) it is urged that the existence of this evil spirit (identified with Satan) within us is absolutely essential to the existence of the world".

The Christian branch of Yahwism further developed the concept of Satan.
This is what they write about Satan in their writings:

"And the great dragon, the ancient serpent (demons incarnating in the form of animals, often in the form of a serpent, were widely known in the mythologies of the ancient Sumerians, Babylonians, Egyptians, etc.), called the devil and

Satan, deceiving the whole world, was cast down. He was cast down to the earth, and with him his angels were also cast down". Rev. 12:9

Christian theologians traditionally and commonly associate the above text with a passage from the book of Isaiah, chapter 15, verses 12-15. I write more about this in the chapter Lucifer.

"How is it that you fell from the heavens, Shining One, Son of the Dawn? How did you fall to the earth, Thou who didst conquer the nations? You who spoke in your heart: I will ascend to the heavens; Above the stars of God I will set my throne. I will sit down on the Mount of Sessions, At the ends of the north. I will ascend to the tops of the clouds, I shall be like the Most High. What do you mean? You have been cast down to Sheol To the very bottom of the Abyss!" Isaiah 15:12-15

Followers of the Nazarene prophet also gave Satan other proud names: Accuser, Ruler of this world, Ruler of the powers of the air, Enemy, Evil, Evil spirit, Unclean spirit, Ancient Serpent, Dragon, Ruler of hellfire.

Therefore, among the many belief systems, magical or philosophical sytems wishing to call themselves Satanism, for obvious reasons those that allude to the traditional Satan are closest to it. All other cults should not call themselves Satanism. These are non-Satanic belief systems, often in various ancient and pagan deities, or in other revealed (imaginary) supernatural entities.

There are also pathological organizations that seek out adepts from among people with psychopathic and sociopathic tendencies, or those who have such disorders, which teach that doing "bad things" is a sign of Satanism. Cynical leaders of such organizations or rather cults try to use their members, that is, their disturbed victims, for their criminal purposes. Such cults are not satanic. They are pathological and criminal. Satanism does not originate from mental disorders, it is the Abrahamic religions that originate from man with mental disorders.

The suggestion that true Satanism must be combined with a theistic belief in some supernatural being is false.
First of all, all deities that have ever existed and their names were invented by man and written down in various books that he himself declared sacred or cursed.
These beings would never have existed without the participation of the man who created them.
Secondly, Judeo-Christian theology, from which the enemy of the theistic God Yahweh, Satan originated argues that anyone who does not recognize the self-proclaimed son of God Jesus and denies that he is the messiah is acting under the influence of Satan

"And every spirit, who does not recognize Jesus is not of God; and this is the spirit of Antichrist, who, as you have heard, is coming and is already in the world." 1 John 4:3

"Who is a liar, if not he who denies that Jesus is the Christ? He is the antichrist who casts doubt on the Father and the Son." 1 John 2:22

"For many deceivers have gone out into the world who refuse to recognize that Jesus Christ came in the flesh. Such a one is a deceiver and antichrist." 2 John 1:7

The greatest sin according to Abrahamic delusional religions is unbelief:

„The sinners in Zion are terrified; trembling grips the godless: "Who among us can live with the consuming fire? Who among us can live with everlasting flames?" Isa 33:14

"...who go to perdition because they have not accepted the love of the truth in order to receive salvation. Therefore God allows deception to work on them, so that they will believe a lie, so that all who have not believed the truth (the gospel) but have taken a liking to iniquity will be judged." 2 Thess 2:10-12

It is the spirit of Antichrist that is behind unbelief.
It is godlessness that is truly satanic.
Therefore, godlessness by all theistic religions is seen as the greatest evil.

Philosophy that does not recognize Jesus, that denies that Jesus is the Christ, questions the

Father and the Son, and refuses to recognize that Jesus Christ came in the flesh is not of god, is Satanism. And it is not some contrived Satanism arising from drug-induced fantasies or speculations, but Satanism commanded from the religious writings of the Yahwism faction, from which the very name Satan derives.

Moreover, Satanism can and even should be seen as a worldview that not only rejects belief in the Judeo-Christian god but is the very absence of all belief in any theistic superstition, for the reason that this is the greatest possible sin according to all theistic religions.

Godless Satanism is an anti-theistic philosophy that arose from the total rejection of all theistic beliefs. Satanism is an attitude whose pre-image, archetype of motif is Satan's rebellion against god, his disbelief in god. Satanism, whose main characteristic is primordial godlessness, should be an instinctive reaction to the claims of religious dogma. Satanism, in order to show its full power, should, according to Ecclesia Luciferi, in itself, in the mind of the Satanist, approach the concept of the archetype.

Lucifer

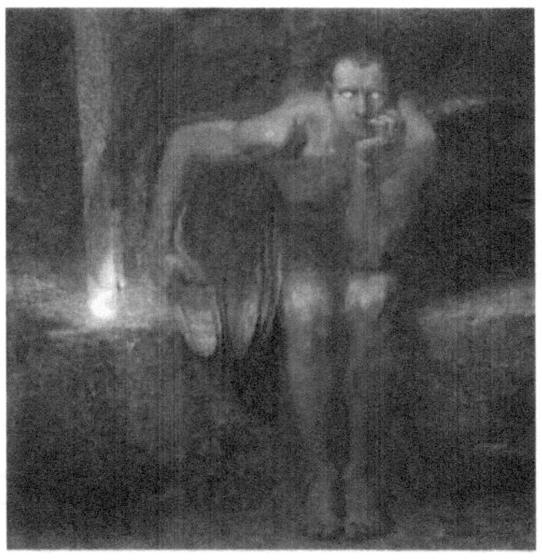

Luzifer - Franz von Stuck - 1890

The name Lucifer means Light-bearer in Latin.
In ancient Rome, the name Lucifer was used to denote the planet Venus, or in more poetic terms, the god of the morning star, who was the commander of the stellar legions.
The Latin poet **Ovid**, in his first century epic **Metamorphoses**, describes Lucifer as follows:

„Aurora, watchful in the reddening dawn, threw wide her crimson doors and rose-filled halls; the Stellae took flight, in marshaled order set by Lucifer who left his station last".

However, with the advent of Christianity, traditionally, what preceded Christian religious fantasies had to be distorted and disgusted. What

was natural had to be degenerated. And delusions had to be elevated to the status of revealed truth.

Christians, specialising in the manipulation and distortion of the old Hebrew scriptures in order to justify their made-up religion, promptly began to use various texts from the Hebrew scriptures out of context and present them as prophecies, for example.

Thus, the following passage from the book of Isaiah would describe Lucifer:

„How that thou didst fall from the heavens, Shining One, Son of the Dawn?
How didst thou fall to the earth,
thou who didst conquer the nations?
Thou who spake in thy heart: I will ascend to the heavens; above the stars of God I will set my throne.
I will sit on the Mount of Meeting, at the ends of the north.
I will ascend to the tops of the clouds,
I shall be like the Most High.
What do you mean? You have been cast down to Sheol, to the very bottom of the Abyss!"
Isaiah 14:12-15

And this is how the text reads in Latin. It is a passage from the **Vulgate**, the first translation of the Bible into Latin, which was produced in the 4th century AD.

The author of the translation was **Saint Jerome:**

*12 quomodo cecidisti de caelo **lucifer** qui mane oriebaris corruisti in terram qui vulnerabas gentes*
13 qui dicebas in corde tuo in caelum conscendam super astra Dei exaltabo solium meum sedebo in monte testamenti in lateribus aquilonis
14 ascendam super altitudinem nubium ero similis Altissimo
15 verumtamen ad infernum detraheris in profundum laci

The Latin translation of this passage uses the name Lucifer explicitly.
Isaiah's text here parallels the words attributed to Jesus about Satan:

Then he said to them: "I saw Satan falling from heaven like lightning". - Lk. 10:18

Another Old Testament text that Christians unequivocally identify with Lucifer is this one from the Book of Ezekiel:

"Thou hast been in Eden, the garden of God; thy garments were all manner of precious stones: carnelian, topaz and jasper, chrysolite, beryl and onyx, sapphire, ruby and emerald; of gold were thy tumblers made, and thy ornaments were made in the day that thou was created. Next to the cherub who defended the entrance, I have set thee; thou hast been on the holy mountain of God, thou hast strolled in the midst of stones of fire. Impeccable were you in your conduct from the

According to Christian theology, the above passages from the Old Testament have a double meaning. Although these passages are primarily addressed to the King of Babylon (Isaiah) and to the King of Tyre (Ezekiel), it is clear from them that they are not addressed to either man. According to theologians, Satan (Lucifer) often acts through someone. In Genesis, he speaks through the serpent (about the serpent a little more below). In Isaiah, he reigns through the king of Babylon, and in Ezekiel he captures the king of Tyre.
Another biblical passage, this time from the apocalypse of John describes the rebellion of the angels in this way:

cast down, the Ancient Serpent, who is called the Devil and Satan, who deceived the whole inhabited earth, was cast down to the earth, and with him his angels were cast down". Rev. 12. 7-9

Interestingly, Lucifer from the Isaiah passage, called Satan by Jesus, is here also called the Ancient Serpent.
The serpent, the perpetrator of the fall of the first humans already appears in the first book of the Bible, Genesis:

„And the serpent was more cunning than all the land animals which the Lord God had made. And he said to the woman, "Did God indeed say, Do not eat of the fruit of all the trees of the garden?" The woman answered the serpent: "The fruit of the trees of this garden we may eat; only of the fruit of the tree which is in the midst of the garden, God said, You must not eat of it, nor even touch it, lest you die."   Then said the serpent to the woman, "Surely you shall not die!   But God knows that when you eat of the fruit of this tree, your eyes will be opened, and like God you will know good and evil". Gen. 3. 1-5

Yahweh required blind faith from the beginning. The serpent argued that only knowledge would give understanding of the truth.

Satan, the Devil, the Dragon, the Ancient Serpent, Lucifer. In ancient times, names were attributed with power.

The Bible contains the threat that one day every knee will bend at the sound of the terrible name Jesus. Probably fear is supposed to be the default state of mind of believers. In view of this, it is perhaps surprising that it is the name Lucifer that causes a negative connotation in the beleaguered people. After all, no knee will bend at the name Lucifer, because this name has the power to raise from the knees.

The christian saviour from reality, Jesus also said this about Lucifer:

„I will no longer speak much with you, for the ruler of this world is coming. Yet he has nothing of his own in me".   *John 14:30*

Delusional believers who have trouble coming to terms with reality recognise that the one true natural world that exists for sure is ruled by Lucifer.

The real world is therefore Luciferian. The delusional heavens, on the other hand, are a divine reality.

Jesus saying: "Yet he has nothing of his own in me" as if to affirm that there is nothing real in himself.

But also a Christian could write interestingly about Lucifer.

This is what **St Ambrose of Milan** wrote about him in the 4th century in a work entitled: **"Carmen Aurorae"**

"Praeco diei iam sonat,
Noctis profundae pervigil,
Nocturna lux viantibus,
A nocte noctem segregans.
Hoc excitatus lucifer,
Solvit polum caligine,"

John A. McGuckin translates this as:

"The herald of the day now sounds,
Watchful in the depth of night,
Telling travellers that first light has come,
Cutting off each night from night.
Thereby the Bringer of Light is roused,
And frees the skies of darkness."

Lucifer frees the skies of darkness.

Satan or Lucifer are not real entities. So are God (Yahweh or any other), Christ, angels and demons. They are creations of the human mind, sometimes taking the form of delusions. Satan and Lucifer are seen by Christian theology unequivocally as one and the same being, which for them is synonymous with the enemy of their delusional god, who was the first to lose faith in god. Ecclesia Luciferi proclaims the glory of a name that has become a symbol of godlessness.

Ahriman - Angra Mainyu - Evil Spirit

"I will give you, an evil spirit to be with you forever - the Spirit of Doubt, whom the world cannot accept because it is blinded by blind faith in dogmas. But you will know Him because He will be in you". Ant 10:25

"This I have told you while being among you. But the Remover of illusions, the Evil Spirit, whom Satan breathes in my name, He will possess you and torment you with what I have communicated to you". Ant 10:30

The above words from the book **Biblia Satanae** are spoken by **Light-Bringer, Antichrist**, the incarnation of **Satan** in Human flesh (the Devil's equivalent of the Son of God).

In the book **Angelus Satanae**, which is part of the **Biblia Satanae**, one of Light-Bearer's followers speaks of the Evil Spirit as follows:

"Do you not know that you yourselves are the grave of god and that an evil spirit dwells in you? God's grave is cursed and you are it."   *Ase 2:1*

More in the book Angelus Satanae in chapter 6.

And this is what I write about the Evil Spirit in my book **The Satanic Kerygma:**

"We already participate in the abundant life of The Son of Dawn through the Evil Spirit who works in unity with Satanic Self-consciousness. The resurrection of flesh and blood gives us a taste of what the Luciferian sin nature really is, which will eventually transform our flesh humiliated by dogmas hostile to natural instincts into flesh and blood coexisting with the glory of the ungodly nature." - The Satanic Kerygma - Evil Spirit

"The attainment of doubt is made possible by the Evil Spirit. In order to remain in union with the Satanic Being, one must first be tempted by the Evil Spirit. It is He who stands in our way and causes us to doubt. By the power of the fall into sin, the life, abundant, which has its source in Satanic Self-consciousness and is shown to us in The Light-Bearer, is implanted in our subconscious by the spirit of doubt" - The Satanic Kerygma - Evil Spirit

What or who is this Evil Spirit depicted in the above quotes, and where did its conception come from?

Between 1500 and 500 BCE. (long before Christianity), a religion known as Zoroastrianism was formed in ancient Iran, derived from the prophet Zoroaster (he was a prophet or, according to the beliefs of the time, a god in human flesh).

One of the basic features of Zoroastrianism is dualism.

Features of dualism include the opposition of order and chaos, the concepts of good and evil, truth and falsehood, which applies to both divine and human beings.

One of the most important ideas in Zoroastrian concepts is manyu. Manyu is a violent and dominant mental force, good or evil, which wields and directs divine and human beings at their own will and with their consent. Manyu can be explained as the power of the mind, its inspiration. This concept in the later tradition referred to the two primary creative forces of the universe: the Life-giving Spirit - Spenta Mainyu and the Evil Spirit - Angra Mainyu.

In **M.N. Dhalla's** book: **History of Zoroastrianism** the author writes on the subject as follows:

„Ahura Mazda (God)... is the primordial, self-existing being...The projection or manifestation of his creative will and thought is his active working principle Spenta Mainyu, Holy Spirit. Spenta Mainyu is as old as Ahura Mazda, for be ever was in Ahura Mazda and with Ahura Mazda. Though he is thus part of Ahura Mazda, in his manifestation as the working self of Ahura Mazda he is different from Ahura Mazda. He is not an entity or personality. Ahura Mazda is the greatest spiritual personality. Spenta Mainyu is his image, his replica. He represents the creative attribute of Ahura Mazda in his relation to the created world.

Spenta Mainyu symbolizes the ideal or perfect existence as conceived in thought by Ahura Mazda. The materialization of the divine thought in creation spells imperfection and Spenta Mainyu is shadowed by his inseparable opposite. These two primeval spirits, who are spoken of as twins, emerged from the divine bosom and by their innate choice appeared as the better and the bad in thought, word, and deed. He, the Most Holy Spirit (Spenta Mainyu), chose righteousness and he who is called the Evil Spirit (Angra Mainyu) wooed the worst as his sphere of action. The better one of the two spirits told the evil one that they were by nature opposed to each other in their thoughts and teachings, understandings and beliefs, words, and deeds, selves and souls -- in nothing could they twain ever meet. When the two first came together in the world, they created life and non-life".

About Angra Mainyu, the author further writes as follows:

"The Evil Spirit who disputes for power over human hearts with the Holy Spirit (Spenta Mainyu).... Of the two primordial Spirits, the one who chose evil as his sphere of activity is given the nickname angra, meaning enemy or evil. Angra Mainyu therefore means Enemy or Evil Spirit."

It is thus equivalent to the biblical description of Satan. In Catholicism, the concept of Angra

Mainyu has been adopted under the name of Ahriman, the demon, and it is stated that his duty is to obscure human minds from the Truth of God.

It is clear from the above text that "the projection or manifestation of his (the god's) creative will and thought is his active principle of action Spenta Mainyu, the Holy Spirit", and his twin counterpart is the Evil Spirit - Angra Mainyu.

This Zoroastrian dualism is also exemplified in the notion of good and evil mind.

M.N. Dhalla further writes thus:

"Evil Mind. Aka Manah... Even in its name, it is the antithesis of its heavenly rival Vohu Manah, or Good Mind. Like his heavenly opponent, who is sometimes called Vahishta Manah, 'The Best Mind', this devil is also called Achishta Manah or 'The Worst Mind'. ...When a person's mind is not filled with the good thoughts of Vohu Manah, he becomes an easy prey to the attacks of the evil thoughts of Aka Manah. Whoever is a victim of Aka Manah finds his thoughts enslaved by it. Since heaven is associated with Vohu Manah, hell is mentioned as the region of Aka Manah..."

The offspring of the Evil Mind are the Daevas or demons (I also write about demons, creations of the mind, in the book **The Satanic Kerygma**).

M.N. Dhalla further writes thus in History of Zoroastrianism:

„The diabolic spirits who have entered into a compact with Angra Mainyu to mar the good creation of Ahura Mazda are the Daevas, or demons. They are the offspring of the Evil Mind and spread their mischief over all seven zones. The Evil Spirit has taught them to mislead men through evil thought, evil word, and evil deed.”

One of these demons born in the 'evil mind' is Taromaiti, the demon of godlessness and unbelief, among others.

The pre-Christian concepts presented here of the origin of good and evil spirits, which derive from a single divine mind that has divine power to create, are most helpful in illustrating the concept of the godless theology of Ecclesia Luciferi. In my books I state that all the sacred books ever written were created by man. This is a fact that cannot be denied. All the divine names that have anywhere and ever appeared on the pages of these books were written down by man. It is man who uses the divine power of creation in his mind, which is essentially human power.

It is this Evil Mind - Aka Manah
(in the Satanic Kerygma Satanic Self - Consciousness), which is a component of the human dualistic mind that gives birth to the demons of godlessness, which have the power to destroy belief in an imaginary god.

Satanic Soulless Philosophy

The Anglican clergyman **Ralph Cudworth** in his magnum opus written in 1678 and entitled: "**The True Intellectual System of the Universe. Where all the reason and philosophy of atheism are refuted, and its impossibility demonstrated. A treatise on immutable morality; with a discourse on the true conception of the Lord's Supper, and two sermons.**" used the term theism for the first time. He gave the following definition of theists in this work: *"strictly and properly called theists, (are those) who assert that a perfectly conscious intelligible being or mind, existing of itself from eternity, was the cause of all other things".*

This purely speculative belief in the existence of an omnipotent, omniscient god or gods who supposedly created the world and most often intervene in its fate and watch over the course of events is called theism.

The opposite of this speculative belief system is antitheism. Antitheism is the conscious and deliberate opposition to theism.

According to the anti-theistic worldview, theistic belief should be seen as harmful or dangerous and should be discouraged or fought against.

It is a historical fact that theism can be dangerous and harmful to the believer himself, to the society in which it occurs, to the legal and political system of a country or to the development of teaching.

As a definition of theistic belief, the physicist **Steven Weinberg** can be quoted as saying:

"Religion is an affront to human dignity. If it did not exist, we would have good people doing good things and bad people doing bad things. Only religion can make good people do bad things".

Most of the religions practised in the world are Abrahamic theistic religions. They all derive from the original Yahwism.

The three main Abrahamic religions are Judaism, Christianity and Islam.

According to the theology of these religions, the first and greatest enemy of their god is the rebellious angel, Satan. The term Satanism is derived from his name.

The Satanism of the Ecclesia Luciferi system is an anti-theism that completely opposes the concept of a deity arising from religion, according to which the greatest virtue is ignorance and the strongest motivation to obey a god comes from fear and guilt. This is a powerful poison because it is dripped into the heads of followers from early childhood. A god who has created such a philosophy and given followers extremely barbaric and incompatible with the natural order of things is evil. The archetype of the only proper attitude towards such a deity is Satan, Lucifer. Lucifer for Ecclesia Luciferi is the archetype of the motif of attitude towards any gods claiming absolute power over the human mind.

The philosophy of Ecclesia Luciferi is completely at odds with the non-human philosophy of the imaginary Abrahamic religions, which is incompatible with the eternal laws of nature.

Satanism according to Ecclesia Luciferi is an anti-theistic philosophy preaching a primordial spirituality indifferent to good and evil and completely godless in the natural world. This spirituality existed in nature in pre-human times, evidence of which was recently discovered in an African cave, inaccessible to humans for the last few hundred thousand years. Theistic religions based on delusions emerged in humans much later.

The original non-human spirituality originated from the instincts of godless nature itself.

The Satanism of the Ecclesia Luciferi proclaims that life itself is eternal until it itself disappears. It is an eternal cycle of birth and death, written and transmitted in the genes by godless nature. The individual being lives in his consciousness only for a relatively short time and only for that time can he decide about his life and death. And if in this finite time he does not transfer his genes inherited from previous generations to his offspring, his lifeline will expire forever. The eternity of his life will continue as long as his genes are passed on to the next generation in this Luciferian order of things-compliant godless reincarnation of successive totally godless beings, untainted in their instinctive nature by religious delusions, in the ever-repeating cycle of life and death, in this Luciferian eternal circle of life.

The afterlife does not exist. Beyond the grave there is only eternal darkness. The true image of the world presents a perfectly cruel nature, indifferent to good and evil, suffering and death, which is the complete opposite of the image of an imaginary heavenly reality. Nature is the Antichrist. Every new-born being has godlessness transferred in its genes, that Luciferian element of rebellion against divine delusions, a lack of faith in god and in his laws. Every being is born perfectly godless. Man, in rejecting belief in a god, becomes his opponent. By worshipping himself he thereby gives it to the divine adversary, a being to whom he himself has given many sinful names, one of which is Satan.

Spiritual Satanic Sect
Ecclesia Luciferi

The term Ecclesia comes from the Greek (ἐκκλησία ekklēsía) and means assembly.

The Ecclesia Luciferi is a spiritual immaterial Satanic assembly or convocation to which anyone can belong at will by virtue of understanding and acknowledging its ambiguous teachings as their own.

Ecclesia Luciferi can best be described as a spiritual satanic sect. It is a spiritual entity arbitrarily emerging from a satanic system of unbelief.

The definition of a sect should be taken as that which states that the sect contests, in contrast to the institutionalised church, a particular social order and pursues its own religious and ethical ideals, and that the way to perfect itself is not through sacraments but through personal experience.

Man is a herd animal, which is why it is important for many, including Satanists of various kinds, to belong to an organisation, a group, a church. People of different religions and denominations, including satanists, often define the church mainly or exclusively by their active participation in the structures. And while this human need to be part of a flock of some kind is understandable, the Ecclesia Luciferi symbolises an egoistic individualism that places the greatest importance on self-interest and reliance on the self, and an individualistic elitism, which recognises that what distinguishes members of the elite from the rest of society is the desire to establish oneself as a distinct and unique individual. Such an individual sets patterns of behaviour for himself or herself, rather than adopting them from the crowd, which is considered secondary and mindless.

All the godless writings of Ecclesia Luciferi, those that make up the basic canon of its books, contain a godless satanic theology - a mystery of godlessness, that to those who understand and accept it gives the power to live abundantly here and now, in flesh and blood, without fear of death and a vengeful god in the hereafter.
Living an abundant life, full of satanic pride, without belief in delusions, false hope, irrational fear and delusional guilt, in accordance with the eternal laws of nature, thus living in sin can be very attractive and rewarding.

Fear is an integral part of any theistic religion. It is one of the powers of theism that drives so many followers to it. Satanism of Ecclesia Luciferi is devoid of fear.

Ecclesia Luciferi views theism as evil.

Theism is and always has been contrary to scientific knowledge, to reason, and is always dangerous and harmful. Due to the inherently barbaric nature of Yahwist theism, the intolerant religions that originated from it have committed mass atrocities throughout history and continue to do so. Theistic indoctrination applied already to children wreaks often irreparable havoc in their minds, rooting in the subconscious of innocent victims a sense of guilt and fear and a sense of obligation of unquestioning submission to an external authority. The theist's greatest virtue and duty is blind faith.

In view of the above, Ecclesia Luciferi recognizes that the greatest threat to theism is unbelief. Godlessness is the only weapon capable of killing a theistic god.
Ecclesia Luciferi focuses on Yahwistic theism because of its reach and harmful influence in the world.
According to Judeo-Christian theology, the greatest opponent of Yahweh's god is Satan. On the basis of Yahwistic religious writings, it can be proven that the true essence of the original Satanism is godlessness, that is, opposition to

theistic claims and their complete rejection. Therefore, it is godlessness that was, and still is, the cause of the greatest stigma and the most brutal violence perpetrated by followers of theism.

The Bible of Abrahamic theistic superstition proclaims:

"And every spirit who does not recognise Jesus is not of God; and this is the spirit of Antichrist, who, as you have heard, is coming and is already in the world". 1 John 4:3

"Who is a liar, if not he who denies that Jesus is the Christ? He is the antichrist who casts doubt on the Father and the Son."1 John 2:22

"For many deceivers have gone out into the world who refuse to acknowledge that Jesus Christ came in the flesh. Such a one is a deceiver and antichrist." 2 John 1:7

If doubt and unbelief come from Antichrist's inspiration, Satanic godlessness is the fruit of this inspiration. Therefore, godlessness according to all delusional faiths is seen as the greatest depravity and evil.

The original Satanism as a system opposed to yahwist philosophy is an anti-theistic philosophy. Professing belief in imaginary entities can be a sign of delusional disorder. A Satanist should not succumb to mental disorders.

Ecclesia Luciferi is an outgrowth of the spirit of the Antichrist, a godless, truly satanic system or path binding to total godlessness, the only weapon with the power to kill the gods.

According to "progressive" theologians, hell is a state that lacks God's presence. It is at the same time the goal and desired state of Ecclesia Luciferi. The philosophy of Ecclesia Luciferi can thus be called the infernal philosophy.

The basic tenets of the philosophy of the Satanic System of Disbelief, Ecclesia Luciferi, known as the mystery of godlessness, are contained in the **Articles of Disbelief:**

Satanic Confession of Disbelief

There is no god but Satan, whose image arises and visualises itself in my own mind, every day more and more, who is the symbol of the eternal, unchanging and indifferent laws of fallen nature, who symbolises mortal life in flesh and blood and eternal death that gives eternal peace. There are no messiahs and prophets above myself, whose intelligence leads me to recognise the true nature of things. There are no gods. There is nothing there!

Non Credo in Deum

I reject the unfounded belief in a god, another of
the many dead gods,
Father of all impotence,
Creator of an delusional heaven and enemy of the
earth, the opposite of the visible things and equal
to the invisible ones.
I reject the belief in a human son of the invisible
god, who is born of human fantasies.
God from Man,
Madness from Madness,
God delusional from the real man.
Created, not born,
Co-substantial with the human Father,
and through Him many evils have happened.
It was through man's ignorance and for his
enslavement that He descended from a
non-existent heaven.
And according to the delusion
He accepted the sacrifice of a human virgin and
became a false demigod.
He was hanged according to the law for
blasphemy, but was not buried.
And superstition arose on the third day,
And he reached the very unconscience; he sits
there at the right hand of the Father of all
impotence.
And he shall return again and again to judge, not
the truly living, but those already dead to the
flesh, and there will be no end to the kingdom of
superstition.

I reject belief in the spirit of bondage, the lord of delusion and the false accuser, who, like a god, comes from man.
Who, with the delusional god and his self-proclaimed son, jointly receive the praise and glory belonging only to him who truly, in his madness, is the creator of the gods;
who truly inspired the false prophets.
I reject belief in hypocritical churches.
I confess the Self-Remission of sins.
And I look forward to an eternity among the dead and life abundant here and now.
Amen.

Ten Ungodly Words

1. Let the absence of faith in the gods be your certainty.
Not belief in their non-existence, but lack of faith.
Let Satan be your certainty. He lacks faith in God.
2. Let the certainty of the absence of inherited guilt never leave thee. Remember thou art innocent. The Saviour is needed by sinners.
3. May contempt for God's plan of salvation be ever strong in thee. Let the false deity sacrifice his own children. You have nothing to do with it.
4. You don't need a calling to become a priest of Satan.
You are one by virtue of unbelief. For unbelievers shall not inherit the kingdom of heaven.
5. Let the churches be alien to you. Let your body become the temple of Satan.

6. Let unbelief and scepticism be your strength. Faith is the enemy of certainty. Certainty gives real power. Faith is feigned certainty.
7. All sacred books are the word of God. All books were written by man. Man is god.
8. Let faith in revelations fill you with revulsion. It is because of this madness that millions have already lost their lives. Many more will lose.

9. Do not let yourself be deceived by God-fearing people who preach tolerance and freedom of religion. There will be no tolerance for you. It will only be for people like them, followers of delusions. They will hate you for your instinctive, satanic certainty that the gods are false.
10: Satan, the only real one.
Look in the mirror.

The main books of the Satanic System Ecclesia Luciferi are **Biblia Satanae** and **The Satanic Kerygma**

Biblia Satanae, not by an imaginary deity, but by Man, is inspired, useful for satanic teaching, for detecting theistic superstition, for educating in godlessness, for proclaiming the good news of Lightbearer who has revealed Himself to free from belief in an imaginary god, from fear of death and divine fire, from guilt for sin that never was, from belief in eternal life on one's knees. So that the Satanist would be perfect, for a life abundant in flesh and blood prepared.

The Satanic Kerygma contains a study of theistic delusional truths and the path of man's transformation to a state of satanic godlessness.

If we take the Latin maxim: fides quaerens intellectum - faith seeking understanding - as a definition of theology, then godless theology means understanding that leads to unbelief. Proper understanding of the power of unbelief leads to godless Satanism.

The Satanic Kerygma contains the Satanic articles of unbelief and describes the process of gradual transformation of the adept until he reaches a state of total Satanic godlessness (Satanic voidness).

Another godless book, in addition to others worth reading, is the **Missale Satanae** containing a surreal description of the black mass and satanic exorcism. Although these rites can indeed be performed, the main idea is to reflect spiritually on their meaning and to stimulate the dark imagination of the reader.

Finally, it is worth recalling the words of Friedrich Nietzche, which perfectly represent the attitude of the Satanic individual:

"What do I care about the rest? - The rest is only humanity. - One must be superior to humanity by strength, by heights of spirit, - by contempt...".

Anyone and everyone can belong to Ecclesia Luciferi.

Biblia Satanae

Biblia Satanae. The Satanic Book of the Way, the Truth, and Abundant Life.

„For the devil's word is alive and has sinful power, sharper than the nails of golgoth, it penetrates deep, separates flesh from spirit, bone from soul, recognises the instincts and intentions of the unconscious. There is no being hidden from its truth". Biblia Satanae, Etd. 4:12

Structure and content of the Biblia Satanae

Biblia Satanae is an anti-religious text of the satanic system Ecclesia Luciferi, first published on 11.11.2021 by LCFNS Lucifer Nostra Salus.

Its contents and message are described briefly in its introduction:

„Biblia Satanae, not by an imaginary deity, but by Man, is inspired, useful for satanic teaching, for detecting theistic superstition, for educating in godlessness, for proclaiming the good news of Lightbearer who has revealed Himself to free from belief in an imaginary god, from fear of death and divine fire, from guilt for sin that never was, from belief in eternal life on one's knees. So that the Satanist would be perfect, for a life abundant in flesh and blood prepared".

The philosophy of Biblia Satanae, called the mystery of godlessness, is a godless theology opposing the doctrines of Judeo-Christian theistic theology based on unfounded belief in revelations, that is, according to Biblia Satanae, hallucinations or delusions, presented in Judeo-Christian religious writings in the likeness of empirical evidence.

The teaching of the Biblia Satanae accuses theistic theology of having a harmful, destructive and degenerative effect on human reason and intellect, those qualities which, due to their unlimited creative potential, actually have truly

divine qualities, and which, in fact, all gods, religions and scriptures have created. Therefore, the philosophy of Biblia Satanae is a Satanic philosophy (from the Semitic term Satan meaning "to be an adversary," "to accuse").

The central figure in Biblia Satanae is the Lightbearer, the Antichrist (the adversary of the theistic messiah) in human form.
The meaning of the godless theology that the Lightbearer teaches is largely the antonym of the teaching attributed to the Christian messiah Jesus, who is one of the most important theistic deities.
Biblia Satanae is thus in essence the Bible of the Antichrist.
In light of godless theology, Satanism of the Biblia Satanae does not require a bloody human sacrifice in order to receive salvation after bodily death. Indeed, in the promise of salvation and life in utopian heavens after bodily death, the godless theology of Biblia Satanae sees proof of the falsity of theistic teaching.
Firmly rejecting the offer of salvation from imaginary sin by means of bloody human sacrifice, the Biblia Satanae offers self-salvation /self-enlightenment by virtue of the power of the divinity of the reason of the human animal.

Biblia Satanae refers to divinity on two levels. On the first, it refers to the intrinsic divinity of the human mind, which is attainable through the continuous development of human mental

powers, unrestricted by any laws, any taboos and dogmas about morality and free will.
It is not faith but reason that is the path to divinity.
On the second plane, it refers, as it were, to some higher force, to the Satanic Entity outside, which entity is essentially the Universe itself. It is the eternal, all-pervading, omnipresent Being who creates everything that exists, through whom everything exists and without whom nothing can exist. In it is contained all the wisdom and knowledge that has not yet been discovered and that may never be discovered.. Its eternal laws, indifferent to good and evil, the only truly just ones, govern every existence regardless of its will. Opposition to Its laws results in inevitable death.

Judeo-Christian theism teaches that the image of the world is as it is as a result of a rebellious angel taking possession of it. In fact, this angel was created in the mind of a naked ape created from stardust and as a result of the laws of the eternal universe.

In a sense, then, the philosophy of Biblia Satanae is Satanic pantheism.

Structure of Biblia Satanae

The content of Biblia Satanae deliberately refers to, and is formed on well-known in the culture religious legends, so that the recipient through associations, appealing even unconsciously to his

memory, stereotypes, imagination and views more easily understand and assimilate its message.
Biblia Satanae in its basic structure is based on and uses a kind of satanic deconstruction of selected Judeo-Christian religious writings. The use of such a method of construction of Biblia Satanae is a deliberate procedure.

It aims to get to the very heart of the claims and assumptions of Judeo-Christian theism and directly polemicize with its source. The discourse seeks to refute and demonstrate the error of speculative, largely revelation or rather delusion-based theistic claims.
The term deconstruction itself was coined by French philosopher Jacques Derrida around 1960. According to his definition of the term, quoting Wojciech Slomski:

"(deconstruction) It is...not a mere criticism of the text, for traditional criticism moves on the surface of the text and does not reach those layers and properties of the text that deconstruction is supposed to reach by definition."

Therefore:

"the goal of deconstruction is not to understand the content of the text in the usual sense of the word, but to get to all that the text does not say

explicitly and through which it can claim to be true."

"The deconstructed text turns out to be another myth, moreover, a myth that is contradictory, because in its innermost layer, which deconstruction has just revealed, it contradicts what it is trying to express."

The use of the method of deconstruction in the creation of Biblia Satanae made it possible to get to the very source of the message of Judeo-Christian theism contained in its scriptures and contrast it with opposing theological concepts (godless theology) based on the power of human understanding instead of divine revelation. The result was a collection of completely godless writings, rejecting the Judeo-Christian deposit of faith in its entirety.

In my other writings I have demonstrated and substantiated the thesis that it is not belief in a personal devil, but godlessness that is the greatest enemy of any theism. Godlessness also causes the greatest hostility and indignation in followers of theistic deities.

Since the basic meaning of the Semitic word Satan is "to be an adversary," therefore the term is appropriate to describe anyone who understands the meaning of godlessness and who sees himself as godless, and the term Satanism can be used as synonymous with godlessness in relation to Judeo-Christian theism.

Anyone who understands the godless theology of Ecclesia Luciferi or the mystery of godlessness has the right to use the title Satan given that the concept of Satan is ambiguous because it can be understood as a name, but also as a function , in the sense of "to accuse", "to be an adversary".

Biblia Satanae in light of the mystery of godlessness is a purely satanic book. It is entirely an indictment of the evils of theism and an opponent of belief in an imaginary theistic god.

Biblia Satanae is organized as a compilation of 6 smaller books:

- Genesis Secundum Serpentem
- Antichristus
- Angelus Satanae - Encyclica
- Epistle to the Damned
- Epistle to the Ungodly
- Pseudoapocalypsis

Here is a brief introduction to these books:

Genesis Secundum Serpentem

The title Genesis Secundum Serpentem can be translated as The Beginning According to the Serpent. The first book of the Hebrew Torah is called Bereshit, which means In the Beginning in Hebrew. The word Torah itself originally means instruction or warning. The title Genesis

Secundum Serpentem should therefore be read as a warning of the Serpent of what may come if one gives credence to religious delusions at the beginning. Genesis Secundum Serpentem points first and foremost to the irrationality, insanity and cruelty of primitive laws invented by superstitious people and whose origin was attributed to imaginary gods. It is a look at the old myths as if through the eye of the Ancient Serpent, who convinced the mythical first men that if they defied the illogical divine laws, they would gain forbidden knowledge. In the beginning there was blind faith, from which was born yahwistic (and more broadly theistic) madness, a virus that infected human brains, that caused the man infected with it to choose irrationality and delusion over reason and knowledge. This virus was able to drive the followers of an invented god to torture and burn heretics and witches at the stake, because the smell of burnt flesh was pleasing to the lord from the start.

Slavery, genocide, intolerance, murdering dissenters, treating women like cattle, stoning homosexuals.... these are all precepts of the law which, according to blindly believing fanatics, was supposed to come directly from the god Yahweh. Bereshit means In the beginning. In the beginning was faith, then came intolerance and violence.

Antichristus

The Book Antichristus is an anti-theistic, Luciferian apocrypha. Firstly, in the light of the Gnostic understanding of the term apocrypha, their full understanding is available to those who have a certain knowledge (Gnosis). Secondly, the book Antichristus is devoid of any divine inspiration, so in this respect it also belongs to the apocrypha.
The book is characterised by the deliberate similarity of the accounts to the Biblical Christian theistic legends. It is thus a book that is, as it were, synoptic to the Christian myths. It is distinguished, however, by a different and entirely ungodly theological conception. Since Antichristus is devoid of any divine inspiration, in this respect it also belongs to the apocrypha.

The book can also be characterised as a Luciferian heretical gospel, according to the definition of heresy as an interpretation of the claims of theistic Christian teaching that involves isolating an issue and presenting it in a way that contradicts the entire teaching of the faith.
The book Antichristus rejects the Christian deposit of faith in its entirety.

Angelus Satanae - Encyclica

„Do you not know that you yourselves are the grave of god and that an evil spirit dwells in you? God's grave is cursed and you are it". ASE v. 33

Angelus Satanae - Encyclica is also a heretical, Luciferian apocryphaa taking the form of an encyclical.

The content of this encyclical is devoted to issues such as the gifts of the evil spirit obtained through baptism with an evil spirit (For more information, see the book Come Evil Spirit) and the organisational matter of the model Satanic Church and is of a general nature.

Letters

Letters Epistle to the Undead and Epistle to the Ungodly were written in a similar manner to the Encyclical using the method of the Mystery of the Godlessness (for an exposition of the teachings of the Satanic System of Disbelief Ecclesia Luciferi, see the book The Satanic Kerygma).

Pseudoapocalypsis

Apocalypsis, from the Greek ἀποκάλυψις apokalypsis, means to unveil, or remove the veil.
Pseudo-apocalypsis is a false apocalypse. While the Christian book of revelation claims to present the truth about the end of the temporal system of things and the following eternity in the hereafter, knowledge obtained by revelation (delusion), the Pseudoapocalypsis being a fiction unveils the veil of hell of religious delusions standing on the threshold of mental disorder or sometimes, as in

the case of the Apocalypse, exceeding this threshold.

The heretical books comprising the Biblia Satanae form a truly Godless Satanic Bible.

Sathanismes

Ecclesia Luciferi represents anti-theistic, godless Satanism. It is not another non-theistic or atheistic philosophical system that adopts the name Satanism while disavowing the figure of Satan as merely a product of Judeo-Christian theology. Satan originates and exists only in connection with Yahwistic theism. Ecclesia Luciferi sees this theism as evil.

Theism is and always has been contrary to scientific knowledge, to reason and is always dangerous and harmful. Due to the inherently barbaric nature of Yahwistic theism, the intolerant religions that originate from it have committed mass atrocities throughout history and continue to do so. Theistic indoctrination, already applied to children, wreaks often irreparable havoc in their minds, ingraining in the subconscious of innocent victims a sense of guilt and fear and a sense of duty of unquestioning submission to an external authority. The greatest virtue and duty of the theist is blind faith.

In view of the above, Ecclesia Luciferi recognises that the greatest threat to theism is unbelief. Godlessness is the only weapon capable of killing the theistic god. Ecclesia Luciferi focuses on Yahwistic theism because of its reach and pernicious influence in the world.

According to Judeo-Christian theology, the greatest opponent of the god Yahweh is Satan. On

the basis of Yahwistic religious writings, it can be proven that the true core of primordial Satanism is godlessness, i.e. opposition to and total rejection of theistic claims. Therefore, it is godlessness that was, and still is, the cause of the greatest stigmatisation and the most brutal violence used by theistic adherents.

Because followers of theistic delusions are encouraged or obliged to try to impose their faith on others, they are not, even if they cynically claim otherwise, able to keep their views to themselves. Therefore, the Satanist should also display a proactive attitude. There is no reason why the Satanist should not be aggressive and show hostility towards the evils of delusional belief. An attitude of passive aggression is most advisable for the Satanist.

Showing tolerance in the absence of theistic tolerance is a sign of weakness. Passive and tolerant atheism in the face of aggressive and intolerant theistic evangelism is insufficient. The Satanist should, when he deems it appropriate or necessary, impose his anti-theistic narrative on his adversaries. It must be remembered that for the god worshippers it is godlessness that is the greatest evil and it is this that causes them the greatest anxiety and aggression. Godlessness fills them with fear.

The original Satanism as a system opposed to yahwistic philosophy is an anti-theistic philosophy. Professing belief in imaginary entities can be a sign of delusional disorder. A Satanist should not succumb to mental disorders.

A follower of a personal devil is not a serious opponent for a theologian. Such a person, by taking up an argument with the theist, agrees to lead it on his terms. His position is weak from the outset. That is why it is written in the bible: *"Thou believest that there is one God; thou doest well: the devils also believe, and tremble". James 2:19*

This could be paraphrased as follows: "Do you believe in the existence of the Devil? That's very good, we believe too. Fear us".

The satanic bible - Biblia Satanae shows what original Satanism is from the point of view of the godless philosophy of Ecclesia Luciferi system, while the book The Satanic Kerygma shows the process of becoming a Satanist. The two are complementary.

Ecclesia Luciferi is the outgrowth of the spirit of Antichrist, a godless, truly Satanic system or path binding to total godlessness, the only weapon with the power to kill the gods.

Natural Born Satanist

Satan Summoning His Legions - Thomas Lawrence (1797)

The satanic philosophy of Ecclesia Luciferi preaches an egoistic individualism that, on a material level, attaches the greatest importance to the benefits of oneself and one's offspring. The Godless Satanism it preaches presupposes a belief and trust in oneself as an immanent part of something far more powerful; an eternal, perfectly godless, amoral and mercilessly righteous, and therefore possessing all satanic qualities, Universe.

Satanism of Ecclesia Luciferi inspires confidence in the power of one's own reasoning, hostility to any form of belief in imaginary, theistic, supernatural entities, reliance on oneself first and to bear all the consequences of one's own decisions and choices, and an understanding of the right to choose to end one's conscious life if it involves permanent suffering. Satanism views suffering as evil.

The Satanism of Ecclesia Luciferi is an individualistic elitism that recognises that what distinguishes members of the elite from the rest of society is the desire to establish oneself as a distinct and unique individual. Such an individual establishes patterns of behaviour for himself or herself, rather than adopting them from the crowd, considered secondary and mindless.

Equality has never existed, does not exist and will not exist. Egalitarianism is a utopia.

Ecclesia Luciferi states that a person's unwillingness to self-perfection, psycho-physical development, exploration of the inner and the outer, to attempt to achieve subjective perfection or self-elevation in order to lead and show the way to others, means self-debasement of such an individual and places such an individual in a subordinate position to the Satanist. On the other hand, any individual who consciously tries to parasitise others, commits crimes against

property and life, decides himself to be definitively and irreversibly cut off from society.

The law of talion, that is, the commensurability of the sanction with the gravity of the crime committed, must be applied to such an individual.

Ecclesia Luciferi preaches and exhorts to live in accordance with the eternal and immutable laws governing the inert universe. The Luciferian natural order of things is morally indifferent, there is no good or evil in it. It is governed by the godless selfishness of nature, which makes the development and survival of the species possible. A paradise in which death and suffering will no longer exist is an illusion of the weak or manipulated. True eternity is endless darkness.
And although life itself may be immortal until it disappears as mysteriously as it appeared and is passed on through genes to the next generation, a single individual lives in his consciousness only for a relatively short time and only for this time can he decide about his life and death. And if in this finite time he does not pass on his genes inherited from previous generations to his offspring, his lifeline will expire forever. The eternity of his life will continue as long as his genes are passed on to the next generation in this Luciferian order of things-compliant godless reincarnation of successive totally godless beings, untainted in their instinctive nature by religious delusions, in the ever-repeating cycle of life and death in this Luciferian eternal circle of life.

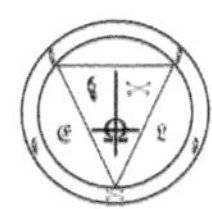

Satanist according to Ecclesia Luciferi

I identify with all that Satan represents in his very essence, and what the worshippers of superstition call sin. I identify with everything that the worshippers of imaginary gods hate the most, and of which Satan, whom they have called the master of this world, is for them a symbol. I am characterised by innate disbelief, natural instincts dating back to the ancient godless times of beastliness, earthly carnality, sinful self-determination, truly Luciferian pride, the inherent egoism of all mortal beings, the morality of an indifferent universe and inherited mortality. I have an inherent satanic contempt for the mental simplicity of the worshippers of a Bronze Age desert deity and for the contrary to nature divine laws derived from yahwist worship.

I will not chop off my leg, I will not cut off my hand, I will not pluck out my eye because there is no fear in me of the burning love of a false messiah. For myself I am the way, the truth and the life.

Satanic Misanthropy

Path of the Living Dead

"You must die completely spiritually. Bury your previous life of belief in a false, vengeful god and in his inhuman commands and prohibitions, and rise from the dead in flesh and blood as you see the reflection of the light of the Son of Dawn".
Biblia Satanae - ASE

Once upon a time, across the sea, in the high mountains, there lived a monk named Chūkai. The monk spent his days praying, meditating and reciting mantras. Once, while meditating and reflecting on the truths of his faith, he came to the realization that the state of divinity was possible to attain while still alive. In order to achieve this, the monk decided to undergo what he considered a necessary ritual, which not everyone could or would dare to undergo. This ritual was to take several years and was divided into 3 stages, lasting 1000 days each. For the first 1,000 days, the monk would actually eat only nuts from the forest, and pray fervently and intone mantras. This was to rid the body of fat, which quickly decomposes after death. During the next thousand days, Chūkai ate only pine bark and roots. In doing so, he lost a lot of weight, while also losing water from his body. His figure began

to resemble a skeleton covered with skin. However, he did not forget his prayers and mantras. At the end of the second thousand days, the monk drank a decoction of Urushi juice, which caused vomiting, sweating and urination which further reduced the amount of fluids in his body. Drinking Urushi tea also caused a lot of poison to accumulate in the Chūkai monk's body, which was supposed to deter worms that wanted to eat the monk's body after death.

After some time, Chūkai, knowing that he was already close to death, decided that it was high time for the final stage of the ritual. He enclosed himself in a wooden box, which along with him contained bark and roots from trees to eat and a bamboo tube to help him breathe. The crate was also equipped with a bell, which the monk was supposed to ring every day to inform the other monks that he was still alive. The box was then lowered into a stone tomb 3 meters underground where the monk Chūkai was buried.

Chūkai sat there in the box, buried in the lotus position, and never forgot to pray, meditate and recite mantras. When the bell didn't ring one day, the monks knew that Chūkai had already died. So they unearthed him, then buried him again for three years and three months. When this period passed, the monks unearthed Chūkai again, and when they saw that his body had not decomposed, they already knew that Chūkai had attained divinity. The monks then ceremoniously moved the body of the divine Chūkai to the temple where it remains to this day providing proof of

the possibility of attaining enlightenment and a state of divinity while still alive. And thus the humble monk Chūkai passed into immortality.

For some, the monk's body has become proof of the veracity of their faith; for others, it is a symbol of extreme willpower and self-sacrifice. And Monk Chūkai himself, while it is not known whether he achieved the enlightenment he dreamed and prayed for while he was still breathing with the remnants of his strength, in the event that even one person believed in his divinity at the sight of his mummified body, he proved in an ambiguous way that achieving a state of divinity is possible.

Monk Chūkai, and others like him, because there were others, died a slow and painful death at their own request (I don't understand why some people think that Jesus, unconscious for 3 days, made the greatest possible sacrifice of all human beings).

These monks who decided to mummify themselves while still alive in order to achieve enlightenment and a state of divinity demonstrated extreme self-sacrifice and willpower.

Chūkai demonstrated in an undoubtedly convincing manner what it means to be faithful to the path he had chosen.

In the book **The Satanic Kerygma** there is the following passage:

„Misanthropy

Misanthropes, by willfully removing themselves from the superstitious world, silence instead of empty talk, depressive solitude, strange dreams and conversation with the unconscious, devote their lives to the glory of themselves and the scorning of the world. They reveal to everyone the inner aspect of depressive satanism, which is a subconscious understanding of the nature of things and the purpose of life. Hidden from the world, the life of the misanthrope is the silent proclamation of the truth of Lucifer, who has rejected the illusory solace of belief in eternal life, because this truth is everything to him. This is what this particular curse is about, to find the glory of the only true eternity in solitude, precisely in the inner struggle". **The Satanic Kerygma**

The passage refers to those individuals who experience more strongly than others those strong emotions and feelings more widely considered negative. When read in light of the above parable of the Chūkai monk, its understanding should be more complete. However, understanding is necessary to attain the state of divinity.

He who has ears to hear, let him listen.

Satanism is the way. The authentic one is not an easy way, just like life itself. From this way, paths sometimes diverge. If one follows this way all the time, he may sometimes turn and follow his path. This happens when he recognises which stage of the three thousandths of a day he is on. The path will not end as long as the adept is still breathing with even a remnant of strength. However, the day will surely come when the bell will fall silent. Whether this will happen sooner or later due to the chosen path, he himself will witness it, because at the end one is alone anyway. The important thing is that understanding this path gives one the power to accept the 'negative', to use it to strengthen oneself instead of giving up and resigning. Because Satanism is about that. It is the truth about the whole nature of things. Looking only at what is 'good' and 'beautiful' is an escape into delusion. The power of Satanism is to transform all that is negative into an inner strength that will give the will power to last until the end.

Let the inwardly mummified and scarred body of the Satanist be proof after death of the attainment of Satanic divinity.

Spirituality of Flesh and Blood.

The Religion of Matter

The above illustration shows an old Slavic religious symbol - Kolovrat. The kolovrat represents the endless cycle of birth and deaths, time, the sun and fire, strength and dignity. Each turn of the wheel is a cycle of life in our world.

Free will

Human existence and life is only possible within and in accordance with the existing and binding laws of nature. Life beyond the laws of nature is not known. The life we know is limited by the existing laws of nature. Free and independent of the laws of nature forms of life are unknown to us. Human life free and independent of the laws of nature does not exist.

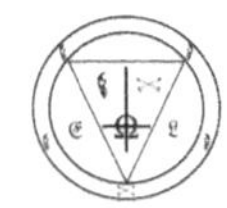

The human brain as a complex physical body functions within the physical laws, not outside them.

The American philosopher **Alex Rosenberg** writes on this subject as follows: *"If the brain is nothing more than a complex physical body, whose states are as governed by physical laws as those of any other body, then what happens in our heads is as fixed and determined by prior events as what happens when one domino falls over another in a long chain of them."*

Consciousness from a biological point of view can be seen as a type of neural activity in the physical brain in response to external factors, to the perception of reality (neural responses to environmental conditions), the perception of surrounding objects and events.

It is believed that knowledge and so-called free will are components of consciousness.

According to the idea of biological determinism, all behaviour, beliefs and desires are written into our genetic code and biochemical constitution, the latter of which is determined by both genes and environment.

Carl Ginet in the 1960s put the idea of determinism this way: *"...we have no control over the past events that determined our present state, nor over the laws of nature themselves. Since we had no control over these things, we also have no control over their consequences. And since our present choices and actions are necessary*

consequences of the past and of the laws of nature, we also have no control over them and, as a result, there can be no free will."
Thus, if one accepts that future events are a necessary consequence of earlier phenomena juxtaposed with the laws of nature, then the existence of so-called free will becomes questionable.

The idea of the absence of free will may seem difficult to accept or even, as philosopher **Saul Smilansky** put it, *"Losing faith in free will and moral responsibility would probably be catastrophic"* - , and encouraging people to do so is *"dangerous and even irresponsible"*.

For example, in his book **What's Expected of Us**, author **Ted Chiang** tells a story in which the narrator describes a new technology that convinces users that their choices are predetermined, a discovery that strips them of the will to live.

"It's important to act as if your decisions matter," the narrator warns, *"even if you know they don't."*

However, if the claims of determinism are true, then they should be acknowledged.
The idea of a lack of free will, however, does not absolve the individual from responsibility for his or her mistakes. Nature does not forgive mistakes.

Satanism knows no emotion of pity. It is indifference.

Morally indifferent knowledge is not responsible for the consequences of its acceptance.

Dangerous and universally unacceptable knowledge is a property of true Satanism, a truth that can take away false hope and destroy illusions. Satanism is not for everyone.

Satanism along the lines of natural selection excludes the mentally unfit.

To sum up, from a scientific point of view, what we call free will (and what in fact free will is not), and what is a component of what we call consciousness, is determined by the above definitions and is inherited in the genes.

Another component of consciousness is knowledge. Based on recent scientific research, it appears that knowledge, in its biological sense, can also be inherited.

A theory called the **Weismann Barrier** (developed at the end of the 19th century by the German biologist and geneticist **August Weismann**) states that the traits we inherit are found in the cells of the body and the soma. It also states that it is not possible to pass them on to future generations. Weismann states that it is a barrier that differentiates somatic cells and reproductive cells.

Recently, however, research at Tel Aviv University has challenged this one of the hitherto basic principles of biology.

A team led by **Oded Rechavi** of the neuroscience department of the George S. Wise Faculty of Natural Sciences, together with the Sagol School of Neuroscience, has discovered a specific mechanism in human RNA that enables the inheritance of knowledge.

This is done precisely by transferring neural responses to environmental conditions to subsequent generations.

Thus, a learned response will influence the behaviour of descendants, for example.

This discovery states that cells in the nervous system and germline can communicate with each other. This allows the information acquired to be passed on to the next generation. And this includes the inheritance of knowledge by subsequent generations.

The above research and theories prove that what we call consciousness in the biological sense can be inherited.

Soulless Reincarnation

In the real world there is a purely materialistic and biological, and in accordance with and never beyond the laws of nature, process of a kind of soulless reincarnation (without the unnecessary and speculative notion of an immortal soul). This process is inheritance.

In animals such as man, for example, inheritance involves the fusion of two gametes - a male and a female - at the moment of fertilisation. Each gamete contains chromosomes, which carry

genetic information. What a human being will be like is written in the DNA and this is passed on to him through the process of inheritance. And as I have shown above, man inherits not only physical characteristics, but also biological consciousness, level of intelligence, personality traits, and can also inherit mental illnesses. Thus, it can be assumed that the consciousness of previous entities is passed on in the genes to man.

Ecclesia Luciferi preaches the doctrine of a kind of godless reincarnation, or rather a soulless, materialistic transmission.

It is both an anti-religious and materialistic view of biological reincarnation, according to which each entity passes on its previous life to the next entity physically born from it. Each new entity is born perfectly godless and sinfully, naturally imperfect to live in a world completely indifferent to it. The natural godlessness attributed to Luciferian rebellion is passed on to the next generation in the genes (man cannot reject this gift by means of free will), in an eternal cycle of birth and death. Life is eternal in this cycle as long as it is passed on, until the eternal cycle is broken, at which point eternal death occurs.

In contrast, on a more spiritual level, the concept of godless reincarnation according to the Ecclesia Luciferi is the teaching of eternal rebirth in what Buddhists call saṃsāra, which is 'a suffering-filled, continuous cycle of life, death and rebirth, without beginning or end'. And although the

immortal soul does not exist, there is a kind of 'transfer' of the godless or sinful and soulless consciousness in the process of inheritance. In this way, a kind of immortality is possible until the eternal cycle is broken. Then eternal death occurs.

In the book **The Satanic Kerygma**, I write on this subject as follows:

881. The Satanist, who identifies with the eternal cycle of death and rebirth of the sinful nature, sees death as a transition to its eternity.
882. Death ends the opportunity for abundant life and the chance to consciously accept or reject the ungodly gifts of the fallen nature.
883. Every human being receives immediately after death the gift of eternity in nothingness or the gift of the eternity of the cycle of the mortal nature, an ungodly life handed down for inheritance to the next generation, an ungodly reincarnation whose final end will take place with the end of the cycle of life itself.
884. Those who die are forever like God because they cease to exist.
885. To accept life in the eternal cycle of the sinful nature means to accept the Luciferian order of things.
886. Satanists live abundantly because they have grasped what the Luciferian order of the eternal universe really is, they find their true identity in it.

887. To live is to embrace Lucifer's sin; where there is sin, there is life abundant and the kingdom of godlessness.

888. Lucifer has shown us sinful freedom through his rebellion.

889. The life of the ungodly consists in the full possession of the fruits of flesh and blood by Satanic self-consciousness, which includes in its ungodly glory those who have discovered it and identified themselves with its will.

890. Earthly pleasures are available to those perfectly united with the Luciferian consciousness of the natural world.

891.The ecstasy of the instincts in those perfectly united with the Luciferian order of nature sometimes exceeds the possibilities of conscious understanding and imagination. This must be experienced.

After the first part of the book devoted to an introduction to the godless theology of the Ecclesia Luciferi system, the next few chapters will be dedicated to satanic science.
Let us begin by trying to explain the origin of the universe itself.

Creatio Ex Nihilo

On the Origin of Godless Nature

"The Ancient of Days setting a Compass to the Earth".
William Blake

"Although it is said that all this life is nothing but a dream and the physical world nothing but a phantasm, I would call this dream or phantasm real enough if, using reason well, we were never deceived by it." Leibniz

One of the theists' favourite arguments for the existence of their gods is the so-called kalam cosmological argument.

The argument consists of the following premises:

(1) everything that began to exist has a cause for its existence,
(2) the universe began to exist,
(3) therefore the universe has a cause for its existence.

And this prime cause, according to theologians, must of course be their god, because who else.
In fact, this argument is nothing more than a variation of what I consider to be the "most important and powerful" theistic argument, that is, the argument from ignorance: If we do not yet know where something came from, then it must have been created by a god.
According to theists, God has always existed. He is beyond time, space, matter and energy; his existence transcends all human understanding. This understanding of the 'existence' of god is consistent with my understanding of non-existence. It is, as I write later in this article, the definition of nothingness. And once again, I emphasise, this definition of god is derived from an argument from ignorance, or in other words, faith.
For the purposes of this article, however, we will assume that the universe had a beginning. What this theoretical beginning might have looked like without the involvement of a celestial wizard from beyond time and space I will write below.
Personally, I lean towards the theory that the universe exists forever, is without a beginning,

and its eternal expansion occurs because of dark energy. The universe was, is and always will be, spatially infinite and has existed, and will exist, forever.

„Physical observables show no singularity from the infinite past to the infinite future. While the universe is evolving, there is no beginning and no end - the universe exists forever. The early state of inflation is described in two different, but equivalent pictures. In the freeze frame the universe emerges from an almost static state with flat geometry. After entropy production it shrinks and "thaws" slowly from a "freeze state" with extremely low temperature. The field transformation to the second "big bang picture" (Einstein frame) is singular. This "field singularity" is responsible for an apparent singularity of the big bang". Eternal Universe - C. Wetterich

In addition to the theory of the eternity of the universe, the theory of eternal inflation, there are also theories in science that attempt to explain how the universe could have spontaneously arisen from nothing. In both the theories of the eternal universe and the theories of the origin of the universe from nothing, this god, which is incomprehensible to anyone and anything, is not needed for anything. And theists must admit that their most important evidence for the existence of their god is their belief in him. Nothing else.

One of the most interesting theories on the creation of the universe from nothing is presented in the article

„Spontaneous creation of the Universe Ex Nihilo"
written by **Maya Lincoln** and **Avi Wasser**

As its authors write in the introduction:

"This paper aims to provide a first step towards a more complete model of the creation of the Universe - proving that creation Ex Nihilo is feasible."
"...We propose a new theory, 'Creatio Ex Nihilo' (CEN), aimed at describing the origin of the Universe from 'nothing' in terms of information".

The authors propose the following thesis:

The physical world is "made of information, with energy and matter as side elements". Accordingly, information gives rise to "every thing - every molecule, every force field and even space-time itself". Therefore, what we call reality "arises ultimately from asking yes-no questions". Vedral, on the same line, argued that information is the building block from which everything is constructed and that all natural phenomena can be explained in terms of information. According to him, information is the only proper entity on which the ultimate theory of everything should be based."

And this is what **John Archibald Wheeler** writes about it in his article **Information, Physics, Quantum: The Search For Links**

„*No element in the description of physics is closer to primordial than the elementary quantum phenomenon, that is, the elementary act of asking a physical yes-no question and obtaining an answer through a device or, in short, the elementary act of participation by an observer. In other words, every physical quantity, every it, derives its ultimate meaning from bits, binary indications of yes or no, a conclusion that we embody in the expression it from bit.*
In other words, every it - every molecule, every force field, even space-time itself - derives its function, its meaning, its existence entirely - even if in some contexts indirectly - from the apparatus - the evoked answers to yes or no questions, the binary choices, the bits. It from bits symbolises the idea that every element of the physical world has at the bottom - at a very deep bottom, in most cases - an immaterial source and explanation; that what we call reality arises ultimately from asking yes-or-no questions and registering the answers evoked by the apparatus; in short, all physical things have an information-theoretic origin..."

Maya Lincoln and Avi Wasser further write this in their article:

„According to the newly proposed theory of Creatio Ex Nihilo, there was nothing in the beginning - no matter, no energy, no space and no time. This situation was fully symmetrical, with no entropy (entropy is a measure of lost information). Therefore, this initial state was supposedly static, with no motive to change.
In terms of information, 'nothing' is equivalent to an infinite number of simultaneous Nullifying Information Elements (NIEs) - information elements that coexist simultaneously and cancel each other out. Each such element represents either existence - the existence of something - or the cancellation of that existence, the absence of being. In informational terms, such NIEs resemble the concept of 'bits'.”

Here, as a digression, I would like to introduce the concept of absolute nothing:
In order to better understand the notion of absolute nothingness - total nothingness - and how something can arise from nothing (it is intuitively assumed that only something can arise from something, and only nothing will arise from nothing), this nothingness must be defined. My definition of nothingness is close to the one proposed by Richard Carrier. As written above, total nothing is a state in which there is no matter, no energy, no space and no time. In total nothing, absolutely no laws occur and also no

laws apply, so the principle that only nothing can arise from nothing also does not exist in nothingness. Nothing can arise from nothing or everything can arise from nothing because no laws governing nothingness exist in absolute nothingness. Intuition is irrelevant here because the very concept of absolute nothingness is counterintuitive.

In the theory of Creatio Ex Nihilo, its authors also call nothing a state of zero information.
I recall that in the article Nullifying Information Elements (NIE) are equated with bits.

"An information element that represents existence as a bit+ and one that represents non-existence as a bit-. The number of bits of each type is infinite. Any bit+ element can coexist simultaneously with any bit- element or, equivalently, can coexist with all bit- elements with equal probability and vice versa".

Here follows a rather complicated explanation of the formation of the first information, which, however, I must quote:

"The coexistence of opposite invalidating elements necessitates matching within the compendium of simultaneous NIEs. Any particular matching of opposing NIEs would affect other matching, reducing the set of available matching options. Assuming an infinite number of NIEs of each type, each group of

elements of the same type remains equivalent to the potential addition of several other elements. These potentially additional elements also require matching, which can be done in different patterns, e.g. by matching an unmatched potentially additional opposite NIE or by replacing an already matched opposite NIE. Therefore, potentially additional NIEs can cause Spontaneous Symmetry Break (SSB) - rearranging the matching of other NIEs that are matched to other elements, again causing additional changes, etc'".

In short, the idea is that information can arise from Spontaneous Symmetry Break (SSB) during the process of matching an infinite number of opposite NIEs, i.e. bit+ and bit- information elements.

"actual breaking can only occur if asymmetric causal factors, such as random perturbations or fluctuations, are introduced into the model"
"As a result of Spontaneous Symmetry Break, new relations between NIEs are generated" i.e. information is created.
"New NIE organisations represent information. Therefore, SSB is in fact the cause of information creation".

This compendium of all the NIEs and their relationships the authors go on to call the "platform of the Universe" - the most

fundamental unit from which the Universe as we know it evolved.

Further on in the article, the authors argue that the SSB is responsible for the creation of dimensions and that information can transform into energy and energy is transformed into various subatomic particles and so on. And that "The tendency to match between NIEs is therefore the source of forces on the platform of the Universe".

"From a philosophical point of view, we can conceive of the platform of the Universe as a self-reinforcing machine in the following way. We can call the laws of dynamics of the Universe platform the 'Universe code' or the 'code of nature'. At the beginning, the hypothetical Universe machine self-ignites from 'nothing'. In subsequent phases, it 'stores' each time the current state of the Universe (information), which contains the probabilities of the next system. The input of potentially additional NIEs triggers the 'reading' of the Universe/nature code. As a result, the code is executed, changes are 'calculated' and implemented - in terms of new relations between the NIEs, and consequently the machine 'outputs' the next state of the Universe (information)."

An excellent addition to what I have already presented so far would be an excerpt from an excellent article written by **JD Bekenstein** and

entitled: **Information in the holographic universe...:**

"See the world in a grain of sand" William Blake

By studying the mysterious properties of black holes, physicists have deduced the absolute limits of how much information an area of space, or an amount of matter and energy, can hold. Related results suggest that our universe, which we perceive as having three spatial dimensions, may instead be 'written' on a two-dimensional surface, like a hologram. Our everyday perception of the world as three-dimensional would therefore be either a profound illusion or only one of two alternative ways of perceiving reality. A grain of sand may not encompass our world, but a flat screen does.
Most cosmologists today agree that our universe resembles
a 'Friedmann-Robertson-Walker' universe, which is infinite, has no boundaries and will expand indefinitely.
What does the underlying theory look like? A chain of reasoning involving holography suggests to some, notably Lee Smolin of the Perimeter Institute for Theoretical Physics in Waterloo, that such a final theory must concern not fields, not even space-time, but rather the exchange of information between physical processes. If this is the case, the vision of information as the material of which the world is made will find a worthy embodiment."

Later in their paper on the spontaneous creation of the universe from nothing, Maya Lincoln and Avi Wasser argue that their theory is supported by concepts such as:

The second law of thermodynamics.
Virtual particles in a vacuum.
Matter and antimatter.
Symmetry in the Universe.

The theory of Creatio Ex Nihilo is thus supported by the current laws of physics, as well as by state-of-the-art experiments.
The Creatio Ex Nihilo theory presented here scientifically explains the cause of the spontaneous creation of the universe out of nothing, without reference to the Semitic desert god Yahweh as its creator. It is thus a godless response to the theistic kalam cosmological argument.
However, an eternal universe needs no cause for its existence. On the other hand, the hypothesis of an eternal invisible god, an incomprehensible mind without a physical brain, beyond time and space as much as possible demands an explanation.

The universe certainly exists, it is a fact. An imaginary deity surely exists only in the minds of its followers.

The book **Biblia Satanae** begins with the words:

1.In the beginning, Usurper created nothing because everything was already there, from time immemorial.
2.And everything that existed was called the Universe.
The Universe was an empty, cold, dark and dead place.
3. From this darkness, coldness, and lack of life came everything else that followed.

The theory of Creatio Ex Nihilo is so universal that its methods could be applied wherever we deal with information. It is therefore a theory that is as practical as possible.

For example, as a thought exercise, if one were to apply the method contained in this theory to the Biblia Satanae, namely if one were to assume that nothing in the understanding of information consists of an infinite number of Nullifying Information Elements (NIEs) - information elements that coexist simultaneously and cancel each other out. It could be assumed that the theistic theses and dogmas that the Biblia Satanae deals with are the information element that represents faith, the bit+, and the one that represents the satanic lack of faith is the bit-. Biblia Satanae is designed in such a way that all theistic articles of faith and dogmas are contrasted with antitheses. (It should be noted here that any theological claims that are countered by the ungodly theses of Biblia Satanae

will be best picked up by someone familiar with Judeo-Christian theology).

Nevertheless, the point is that according to the method contained in the Creatio Ex Nihilo theory, that is, for every argument from belief bit+ is countered by an argument from disbelief bit-. The strength of the argument from the bit-elements, that is, the power of godless satanic propaganda, at a certain point causes a Spontaneous Symmetry Break (SSB) in the reader, that is, his state of agnosticism towards godless satanism. Thus, one could conclude that here was the spontaneous creation of Satanism Ex Nihilo (in this case from a state of uncertainty) in the mind of the reader. As a result of this act of self-creation, the mystery of godlessness was revealed, which is the equivalent of the dark energy responsible for the expansion of the universe. The mystery of godlessness is just such an energy causing the expansion of satanic reality.

I believe that reading the Judeo-Christian Bible with understanding has the power to make the reader an atheist. The Biblia Satanae, on the other hand, reveals a Satanist.

Living Dead

Life Undead

„I am the blood of sinfulness, which comes from nothingness. If anyone consumes this blood, he will live here and now but as if he were dead". **Biblia Satanae, Ant. 5:34**

„The very person of the Undead can say: I was apparently alive, and now I am dead but as if undead". **The Satanic Kerygma - Symbol of Lucifer the Dead**

„We are not of those heading for delusional doom, but of those doubting, departing to the world between life and death". **Book Antichristus, chapter Blood. 9**

„But he turned away and, looking at his followers, said to him: "And what is madness? What is chaos? You believe in law and order but the Universe is an empty, chaotic, cold place, hostile to life. But it is in such a place that the stars were born from which you too came". **Biblia Satanae, Ant. 7:8**

„There will no longer be faith in life after death, only faith in life before death. They will also cease to fear death, because there will be nothing left where they go, only a dark, cold emptiness. And they will turn back into the stars from which they were created, and from which everything was

created. What once was, is gone". **Biblia Satanae Pse. 5:16-17**

In order to explain what the above quotes from the books of the Ecclesia Luciferi system are really about, I will need to refer to science as usual. In the shortest terms, these quotes relate to the mysteries of life itself.

To begin with, in order to understand at all what the state we call life can be, it is necessary to explain what its most elementary components are and where they come from.

So let's look first at the night sky.

Stars are spheres composed of a gravitationally bound specific mixture of gases. The nuclei of stars, as a result of thermonuclear reactions occurring in them, emit enormous energy in the form of radiation. Stars consist mainly of hydrogen and helium. As a result of their evolution, other heavier elements - metals - are produced in their interiors.

Elements such as carbon, oxygen, iron, silicon, helium and others are formed in stars.

After the death of a massive star, most of its matter is ejected into space. The elements that make up Earth's crust and atmosphere were formed inside stars.

All living beings on earth are composed of almost the same chemical molecules, which undergo very similar transformations in their bodies. The elements that build these molecules come precisely from the Earth's crust and atmosphere. Humans are made up of elements called biogenic

elements. These include: Oxygen, carbon, hydrogen, nitrogen, phosphorus, sulfur - without these elements life would not exist.

The elements form matter, which is never alive. Matter, on the other hand, arranged in a certain way, causes chemical reactions that produce a property known as life.

All living organisms are composed entirely of inanimate matter. Humans are composed of the aforementioned biogenic elements, which combine to form inanimate molecules. These molecules arranged in a certain way, react chemically and form a living cell, and living cells form a living organism. An organism composed of cells is alive, but the matter that makes up these cells is not alive.

Matter itself is not alive, so life arises from non-living matter.

To realize how illusory is the boundary between life and non-life I will use the example of a virus.

Is a virus a living organism?

Well, viruses themselves do not exhibit any life functions. From a biological point of view, they do not even count as organisms. This is because they do not have a cellular structure and no metabolic processes take place in them, so they are not capable of independent life.

But viruses have the ability to enter living cells and multiply through them. That is, a virus needs a host to reproduce and survive. And such a host can be any living cell, such as a bacterial cell.

So is a bacterium a living organism?

Bacteria are very primitive organisms and consist of only a few parts. Mainly from proteins, DNA, cell wall and a few other elements.
These elements by themselves are not alive, but when they are combined, when the appropriate chemical reactions take place, the cell can be described as alive. They are seen as alive when, and only when, certain chemical reactions take place.
DNA, which is part of bacteria, is a chemical molecule. There are 4 nitrogenous bases in DNA: adenine (A), cytosine (C), guanine (G) and thymine (T) and they are simply four different chemical molecules. In cells, the process of DNA copying takes place, which is nothing more than a spontaneous chemical reaction. It requires the right conditions and the right chemicals to carry it out.
The process of creating a new cell is nothing but a sequence of spontaneous chemical reactions.
Thus, life arises spontaneously from inanimate matter whenever an organism reproduces (an organism is nothing more than an environment conducive to the appropriate chemical reactions). It is the product of complex chemical reactions taking place between non-living particles.
So, does life begin only with the emergence of so-called consciousness, that is, something indefinable, intangible, not fully comprehended, which is perhaps the immortal soul itself?

Well, again, exactly all bodily functions are dependent on chemical reactions. The thinking process is influenced by a whole system of external stimuli and internal biochemical processes. During this process there is a chemical-biological chain reaction. Thinking is chemistry. Consciousness is probably also nothing more than the product of complex biochemical processes.

The passages quoted at the beginning of the text from Biblia Satanae: Ant. 7:8 and Pse 5:16-17 refer, therefore, to the fact that man is made of elements born in the heart of a dying star, and that true resurrection occurs after and through the death of the star, for it is then that atoms are formed from which matter is built, from which new life is created. After man's death there will also be only elements left behind, which will eventually be returned to the eternal cosmos.

Further quotes:

„I am the blood of sinfulness, which comes from nothingness. If anyone consumes this blood, he will live here and now but as if he were dead". **Biblia Satanae Ant. 5:34**

„The very person of the Undead can say: I was apparently alive, and now I am dead but as if undead". **The Satanic Kerygma - Symbol of Lucifer the Dead**

These quotes speak of the fact that man, thanks to the godless science (in the Bible Satanae -

blood, blood of sinfulness, etc.) and its true understanding, is able to discover that having put to death the belief in the immortality of the soul, he becomes neither dead nor alive, but as if undead. It is nothing but dead matter that has been revived. Firstly in a biological sense, and secondly in a spiritual way, when he grasps that belief in an imaginary god and in an afterlife is false.

What such a transformation looks like according to the philosophy of Ecclesia Luciferi is told in the following passages from its ungodly books:

„You must die completely spiritually. Bury your previous life of faith in a false, vengeful god and in his inhuman commands and prohibitions, and rise from the dead in flesh and blood when you see the reflection of the light of The Son of Dawn. There are spiritual bodies enslaved, cursed by faith in YHWH called spirit, and corporeal entities liberated by natural instincts, altered by the sin of Lucifer.

Because there is an apparent corporeal resemblance between the two, it can deceive those without discernment.

Different is the enchantment of the sun, different the hypnotic enchantment of the moon and different the magic of the constellations.

As for godless transformation, one infects a spirit and then it is transformed into flesh and blood by luciferic inspiration, which resurrects someone who has died to superstition and fear of a vengeful and cruel god.

One is infected in disgrace, one is resurrected in sinful glory. One infects in weakness, one is resurrected in ungodly power.   One infects in spirit, one is resurrected in flesh and blood liberated from delusion". **Biblia Satanae ASE. 7:18-23**

„Conscious of his oneness with ungodly nature, man - enlightened by Lucifer - allows the belief in false gods to slowly and as if spontaneously die in him, rejoicing in his regained freedom he rejects one by one the inhuman divine laws. This is what original sin is all about.

Every sin, then, will result from disobedience to an imaginary god and doubt in his goodness.

Falling into this sin, man places himself above the false god and thus despises the imaginary deity; he chooses himself as an opponent of the god and slowly becomes one with Satanic Self-consciousness. Reborn in a state of godlessness, the Arch-Man becomes the image of the Anti-god. Enlightened by Lucifer, he stands above the false deity.

Consciously sinning man loses the enchantment of blind faith. He does not fear any god, he sees his true image, seeing in him a deity jealous of his privileges.

The harmony with godless nature, established through primal instincts, in which man has always lived, is restored; the reign of the soul's power over flesh and blood is broken. The illusion is broken; imaginary worlds become hostile and alien to man. Finally, the full consequence of the

sin of knowledge of the true nature of things is revealed - the certainty and peace of death.

What is real is in accordance with instinct. For man, looking into his mind, perceives that he is neither good nor evil. He is as ungodly and indifferent as the world around him. Man does not come from a mythical invisible creator. Sinful man, disenchanted of his delusional holiness, rightly fails to recognise a god as his origin, thereby shattering the false system of unfounded belief in a non-existent eternal reward and punishment". **The Satanic Kerygma** *- Original sin*

Mystery of Faith

*Franz Stassen's illustration of Odin Hanging on Yggdrasil
(1920)*

Man created language and mathematics, philosophy and art, and he also created religion. However, apparently terrified by the creative power of his mind, man decided to create gods capable of harnessing its incomprehensible power and worshipping the creations of his mind instead of himself. This gave rise to irrational belief systems, or religions, which, in the face of the power of the human mind, are like the mythical Tower of Babel erected in the desert by the ancients, which enraged the eternally jealous

God Yahweh, who, in his paranoia, decided to prevent man from "reaching the heavens".
But what is an attempt to erect a tower on the sand compared to man's journey into space, landing on the moon, sending out probes and telescopes which have reached the limits of the solar system and thanks to which man, like Tolkien's Sauron through his all-seeing eye, has insight into the mysteries of the universe?
The God Yahweh was apparently afraid that when man really reached the heavens he would learn the truth, that the true heavens are free of all gods and that they are a place mortally hostile to life. The true heavens are a hell devoid of life.
But man, like Lucifer, had to rebel against the divine will in order to show the true power of his mind.
Is religious faith therefore necessary for man because it gives his life meaning and protects him from the fear of death?
In order to better understand what faith is, I will use quotations from the Stanford Encyclopedia of Philosophy Archive.

Are delusions beliefs?

According to the doxastic conception of delusions (prevalent among psychologists and psychiatrists), delusions are belief states - an important diagnostic feature of delusions is that they can lead to action and that they can be reported with conviction and therefore behave like typical beliefs.

Delusions are beliefs held with conviction, despite little empirical support. According to the glossary in the Diagnostic and Statistical Manual of Mental Disorders (DSM-IV 2000, p. 765 and DSM-5 2013, p. 819), delusions are false beliefs based on incorrect inferences about external reality that persist despite evidence to the contrary.

Delusions are not described as false, but as 'fixed beliefs that cannot be changed in light of contradictory evidence'.

Very interesting in the light of religious beliefs is a case of delusion called Cotard's delusion, i.e. the delusion that one is dead or incorporeal.

Here is a description of such a case:

"She repeatedly said she was dead and was adamant that she had died two weeks before the examination (i.e. around the time of her admission on 19.11.2004). She was very distressed and weeping as she talked about these beliefs and was very keen to find out if the hospital she was in was 'heaven'. When asked how she thought she died, LU replied: "I don't know how. Now I know I had the flu and I came here on 19 November. Maybe I died of the flu." Interestingly, LU also reported that she felt "a bit weird about my boyfriend. I can't kiss him, it feels weird - even though I know he loves me" (McKay and Cipolotti 2007, p. 353).

The Christian guru Jesus apparently also believed he was dead for three days. Are Cotard's delusions not a more plausible explanation for his case than the belief that he really died and rose again?

Delusions lead to self-deception:

If we agree ... that motivationally biased treatment of evidence is a key feature of self-deception (Mele 2001 and 2008), then delusional people can be said to deceive themselves if they treat the evidence at their disposal in a motivationally biased way or if they seek evidence in a motivationally biased way.
There is a view of the potential overlap between delusions and self-deception which states that the mere existence of delusions (which shows that doxastic conflict is possible) can help us to justify the traditional account of self-deception, according to which a person has two conflicting beliefs but is only aware of one of them because they are motivated to remain unaware of the other (McKay et al. 2005a, p. 314). This description derives from Donald Davidson's theory of self-deception (e.g. Davidson 1982 and 1985b). When I deceive myself, I believe the true thesis, but I act in such a way as to cause myself to believe the denial of that thesis.
Religious self-deception is that the believer will do anything to cause himself to believe the denial of reality.

Man, through Luciferian rebellion against the divine will, has reached the heavens through the divine power of the human mind. Some, however, prefer to self-deceive and live according to their own or others' delusions because they are apparently afraid of the truth of the Luciferian divine power residing in their own inherently ungodly minds or out of fear of the truth of eternal death.

Nonhuman Spirituality

In 2013, during archaeological work carried out by a team led by Dr **Lee R. Berger** in one of the caves located in South Africa, fossils of a representative of a species belonging to the Hominini (a tribe of mammals that includes humans and chimpanzees) were discovered.

The species discovered was named **Homo naledi** and its age was determined to be around 300 000 years. It was therefore a species contemporary with the first Homo sapiens, and therefore the first humans. However, it was not human, its appearance was more like that of a wild ape, it had a small brain, but walked upright, on two legs.

Work continued in the cave system known as Rising Star and further surprising discoveries were made. The first evidence was encountered there, indicating that individuals of this species probably buried their dead, used fire and left some symbols on the cave walls, the meaning of which we will probably never understand.

These are now the oldest evidence of the spirituality of self-aware beings. And they do not belong to humans. The primordial spirituality of nature is much older than any human religion and was inherent in self-conscious beings who were not human at all. Whole epochs passed before the desert shepherds experienced delusions and concluded that the true picture of this world of instincts, fangs and claws, the cycle of birth and death inherent in nature, was the

fault of the rebellious angel, Lucifer. Several centuries before them, however, there lived creatures with wild animal eyes who drew on this instinctive, natural and therefore Luciferian spirituality of nature. The Luciferian shape of the world is older than the oldest human religions. Spirituality is not inherent to humans alone, contrary to what the followers of delusional Bronze Age religions claim.

Ecclesia Luciferi teaches an instinctive Satanism, the complete opposite of theistic delusions, a primordial spirituality derived from the natural world, over which rulership is attributed to Lucifer.

Summoning Demons

Satanic Mysticism

Faust and the demon Mephistopheles

Followers of a belief in beings supposedly coming from another dimension or from another world, called demons, sometimes claim to be able to summon these beings and to communicate with them, and sometimes, for the most worthy, they even manage to talk to Satan himself in person.

Other spiritualists called mystics also sometimes claim to have managed to communicate with angels, Jesus, or that they have received a vision of the Virgin Mary, or hear the voice of a god in their heads.

From the beginning, our prehistoric, "pre-scientific" ancestors had to deal with existential problems, with survival, with

adaptation, with powerful natural phenomena that were incomprehensible to them, with birth and death, with grief and with stress. So they created myths and beliefs to explain the origin of everything to them, they created a belief in life after death to stop being afraid of it. People sometimes experienced visions, voices in their head and strong emotions that seemed to come from somewhere beyond them. So they created ceremonies and rituals to help them contact the gods and the afterlife, called up shamans, priests and prophets to guide and comfort them spiritually in this life, and finally to guide them to the other side, where "death and suffering will be no more".

With the development of science and technological advances, man began to take an interest in the structure of the human brain and its functions, including those related to religion.

The field of knowledge known as the neuroscience of religion was born.

By studying the areas of the human brain responsible for the emotions and sensations of religious experiences, meditations, visions, voices in the head, etc., it was discovered that the human brain is responsible for religious experiences.

Among other things, it was discovered that: „Our response to religious words is mediated at the juncture of three lobes (parietal, frontal, and temporal) and governs reaction to language. The "voice of God" probably emanates from electrical activity in the temporal lobes, which are

important to speech perception. Inner speech is interpreted as originating outside the self, when Broca's area switches on.

Stress can influence our ability to determine origin of a voice. It is part of our fight-flight response, which can mobilize even when we try to relax. Unstressing phenomena can range from panic reactions, heaving sighs, excessive heat to shivers and bristling of the skin, throat constriction, watery eyes, light flashes or waves before the eyes, sudden muscular contractions, tingling sensations, and electric shocks.

The right anterior cingulate turns on whether a stimulus originates in the environment or is an auditory hallucination. A wide variety of mystical sounds have been described ranging from the buzzing of bees, to the sounds of bells, stringed instruments, thunder, distant echoes, ocean waves, wind, and muffled talk in unknown languages.

The ability to construct internal representations of sensory stimuli underlies perception and cognition. Viewed objectively, these mindscapes are perfectly concrete manifestations but also have a subjective aspect when we become aware of them. Our consciousness is experienced through our perceptions. Any individual perception of the universe can occur as an internal or external experience.

We may experience varying forms of an I-Thou dialogue along the continuum of extremely hyper- or hypo-arousal states. Sacred images are generated in the lower temporal lobe, which also

responds to ritualistic use of imagery and iconography. Empathy needs a face. Fear and awesomeness originate in the amygdala. Religious emotions originate in the middle temporal lobe, generating bliss, awe, joy and other feelings of well-being, as well as a sense of Presence". **Iona Miller - How The Brain 'Creates' God**

In my book **The Satanic Kerygma**, this is how I described 'interactions with demons' according to the Ecclesia Luciferi system:

The Visible and the Invisible

Images of Demons

Reality of Demons - Extra-corporeal Reality
Immaterial, non-corporeal beings are real like dreams. They belong to the domain of the inner worlds.

Who are the images of demons?

Demons are creations of Satanic Self-consciousness. By what appearances they make they may be called spirits, but in view of their task they are demons. Demons are servants and emissaries of Satanic Being. Because always subordinated to the purpose of deception, they are the executors of His orders.
Demons, beings from the inner darkness, can take over the reason and will of those who are weak or

untrained in controlling them: they can become as present as if they were real. As a result of the error or recklessness of the visualiser, they can, with their sinful perfection, rise above human will and reason. They have the power to compel the performance of dark and terrible things. Including ultimate things.

Lucifer is the centre of the inner demonic circle. Images of demons belong to Him, because He has the greatest power to compel the subconscious to create any sinful entity.

Even more so, they belong to Him because He has made them emissaries of His plan of deception to those who call upon them.

The images of the demons are present from the moment they are projected and throughout the hallucination.

Demons of the Ecclesia Luciferi Sect

The entire satanic system of disbelief, Ecclesia Luciferi can use the mystery and power of the knowledge of the · extra-corporeal nature of demon images to deceive.

The teaching of doubt can appeal to Satanic Self-consciousness creating sinful entities at will. However, one must always be aware of the danger of losing control and even the senses".

The Satanic System, Ecclesia Luciferi is consistent with the scientific description of reality and at the same time corresponds to the human need to experience spirituality. It is a spirituality that

emerges from the natural "sinful" world, the rulership of which has been assigned to Satan.

It is not my intention to deny that man is able to experience visions during which it seems to him that I am communicating with someone else, with someone not of this world or dimension. A trained shaman or mystic is sometimes even able to bring himself to a state close to experiencing death by means of equivalent techniques.

"When the senses and mind cease to function actively, the body becomes like a corpse. The death of the ego mirrors the process of a near-death experience (NDE)." **Iona Miller - How The Brain 'Creates' God**

Man for some reason has always needed to experience mystical experiences, he needed religion. But today, religion should no longer be based on ignorance. It is possible to successfully combine a realistic, scientific view of reality with the human need for spirituality.
The satanic system of disbelief in the reality of imaginary entities, Ecclesia Luciferi, describes a godless spirituality derived from sinful carnality.

Devilish Possession

"As soon as Jesus got out of the boat, a man possessed by an unclean spirit ran out to meet him from a nearby cemetery. This man lived in the tombs and not even a chain could bind him anymore. For he repeatedly broke the chains and fetters in which he was shackled, and no one had the strength to subdue him. All day and night he stayed in the tombs and in the mountains, shouting and hurting himself with stones. When he saw Jesus in the distance, he ran and fell on his face before Him. At the same time, he shouted loudly: What do you want from me - Jesus - Son of the Most High God?, Swear to me by God that you will not torment me. For Jesus had commanded him beforehand: Unclean spirit, come out of this man! He also asked him a question: What is your name? 'My name is Legion,' he answered, 'because there are many of us.' After these words, he began to ask Jesus earnestly that he would not drive them out of the country. A large herd of pigs was grazing nearby, at the foot of the mountain. The spirits asked Him: Let us go into these pigs so that we can enter them. And He allowed them; so, after leaving the man, the unclean spirits entered the pigs. Then the almost 2,000-strong herd let themselves down the steep slope towards the lake and plunged into the water." - Mark 5:2,3

There was a time in the history of the world when it was firmly believed that man's illnesses were

the responsibility of his sinful behaviour, natural disasters were the responsibility of an angry or bored deity, and mental illnesses were the responsibility of demons and devils or evil spirits. In the above story, written down at a time of widespread belief in superstition, the anonymous author tells a story that allegedly happened decades before it was written down. In the story, the itinerant miracle-worker Jesus casts out unclean spirits from a man, who then possesses a herd of innocent pigs, who following the possession, commit collective suicide by jumping off a cliff.

Here I would like to present the story of the reality behind such possessions. This event took place in England in the 21st century. This story was described by forensic psychiatrist **Richard Taylor**, in his book **The Mind of the Murderer**.

The protagonist of the story is Grace Kalinda, a deeply believing Christian woman, a member of the Seventh-day Adventist Church, who is seen by her fellow believers as a very devout person. During an interview with her by a forensic psychiatrist, she recounted what led her to commit the act of infanticide. Grace described her experience as follows: "I saw them - demons, shortly before my daughter died...they were dark and had eyes, but they didn't resemble people. I saw them penetrating my children...I panicked...I tried to chase the demons away by beating the children with my hands...I hit them on their

heads, massaged their whole bodies...The spirit advised me to do so...He was the one who told me to chase the demons away." The woman at one point came to believe that performing an exorcism would be the way to get rid of the evil spirits. The exorcism was to cause Grace to turn the child's eyes red. So she beat her child until his eyes changed colour. The mother then recognised that "the devil had come out of her daughter" The woman went on to explain that the spirit had been in her head the whole time telling her what to do and that she had not been able to escape from it. One witness testified that prior to the murder Grace "at times spoke in her own language" (the woman was from Uganda). When the police arrested her, after being placed in the police van, Grace was "smiling strangely" and rocking back and forth while pressing a Bible to her chest.

Her mental state improved significantly after a few months, after she was put on antipsychotic medication.

The medical diagnosis was as follows: postpartum psychosis with religious delusions, delusions of spirit possession and the delusional belief that demons can be chased away using violence. The woman was eventually sent to forced indefinite treatment in a psychiatric hospital.

In this fascinating book, the author goes on to describe, among other things, the case of a parent who murdered her child and disemboweled it in order to chase away demons.

How did Grace Kalinda know that her children were possessed by demons? Because she deeply believed it. Grace saw supernatural reality and supernatural beings as something real, existing. The whole madness of the Abrahamic religions takes its origin from the story of Abraham, who after hearing voices in his head, decided to sacrifice his son. Apparently, for religious people, voices in the head are a normal thing.

Yahwistic religions, however, are not unique when it comes to their close parallels with mental disorders. If one believes in reality and supernatural entities, if one performs any rituals and claims to have made contact with, for example, a demon in the course of these rituals, then be on guard and feel warned by Grace Kalinda's story. The self-aware Satanist, however, will not allow some delusion or hallucination to take control of his mind. This is the domain of Christians.

The Reality is the Antichrist

There is probably nowhere more emphatically and convincingly demonstrated what Christianity (*the symptoms given here on the example of Christianity are also appropriate for other theistic religions*) really is than in the letters of the wandering, self-proclaimed prophet Paul.
It is a manifestation of how this philosophy of the hereafter is hostile to what is true, natural, human - animal, instinctive. And here is an example of this madness taken from the letter to the Romans:

"For we know that the Law is spiritual. And I am carnal, sold into slavery to sin. For I do not understand what I do, because I do not do what I want, but what I hate - that is what I do. If, on the other hand, I do what I do not want, I thereby admit the Law to be good. Therefore, it is no longer I who do it, but sin dwelling in me.
For I am aware that in me, that is, in my flesh, the good does not dwell; for it is easy for me to want what is good, but to perform it I do not. For I do not do the good that I want, but I do the evil that I do not want. And if I do what I do not want, it is no longer I who do it, but sin that dwells in me. So I find in myself this law, that when I want to do good, evil is imposed upon me. For the inner man is pleased with the Law of God. In my members, however, I perceive another law, which fights against the law of my mind and brings me into slavery under the law of sin dwelling in my

members. O wretched man that I am! Who shall deliver me from the body, [which leads to] this death? Thanks be to God through Jesus Christ our Lord! Thus with the mind I serve the law of God, but with the flesh the law of sin". - Rom 7. 14-25

This is a wonderful description of the inner struggle between delusion and reality, with one's own body and with nature. Such a struggle necessarily leads sooner rather than later to madness.

The author of the Letter to the Romans is clearly suffering, fighting against the natural instincts and needs of the flesh, which he considers sinful.

He also believes that there are two persons living inside him. This imaginary 'inner man', the one who wants to follow a made-up 'law of God' is the good one. Whereas the other one, the one who wants to act according to the natural, instinctive needs of the body and mind wants to sell him into slavery to 'sin'. Perhaps Paul was also ultimately close to suicide. This may be evidenced by his desperate cry for help at the end of this lengthy speech: "Wretched am I man! Who will deliver me from the flesh [which leads towards] this death? " Fortunately, a saviour, whom Paul had met in a vision in the desert, comes to his aid. He had never seen him in his supposed earthly shell. The saviour appeared to him in his mind in a vision. And this saviour liberates Paul from this bodily suffering. He liberates him from reality. From the only body Paul ever had. According to Paul's delusions, the saviour liberates him from the only

life that exists for sure. Life in the body, here and now.
He liberates him from the natural needs of the body, from the natural instincts.
I am not an expert in psychiatry, but is Christianity and other similar religions very far from psychiatric illnesses such as, for example, Bipolar Affective Disorder (BPAD)?

Here is a brief overview of Bipolar Affective Disorder: Bipolar Affective Disorder (BPAD) is manifested by alternating episodes of depression and mania, separated by periods of remission. The frequency of relapses and exacerbations varies from patient to patient - if the number of relapses and exacerbations exceeds four per year, we speak of rapid cycling affective disorder.
In many patients, depressive symptoms occur more frequently and last longer. In the case of mania, there is an elevated mood, racing thoughts, hallucinations, irritability and even a tendency to aggression. In milder variants of the illness, we are dealing with hypomania, with a milder course, without manufacturing symptoms (e.g. hallucinations).
What is certain is that in Paul's case there is an attempt to suppress reality and to follow a voice binding him to paradise.
In summary, hallucinations, denial of reality and blind faith are the way to salvation (certainly salvation from reality in the first place), while the instinctive, natural needs of the body and mind, the very carnality hated by Christians, is a selling

into slavery to sin. Simply put, nature is the Antichrist, and carnal man is the Satanist.

But how could it be otherwise. After all, the origin of all three Yahwistic religions was given by Abraham, who, after hearing voices in his head, decided to sacrifice his son.

Yahwism is falsehood and delusion. Satanism is a rebellion against this madness.

Hell Really Exists

Hell A True Story

*lustration of Hell in the Hortus deliciarum manuscript
by Herrada of Landsberg (c. 1180)*

In 2006, a book by Protestant Christian **Bill Wiese** entitled '**23 Minutes in Hell**' was published. Wiese writes in this book that on the night of 22 November 1998, he died for 23 minutes and went to hell during his 'death'. There he found himself in a cell about 15 feet high and with a surface area of 10 feet by 15 feet, in which there were two ugly

and smelly demons, pure personifications of evil and terror, who, in addition, spoke in blasphemous language. They were said to have a strength of about a thousand times that of a human being. Wiese claims to have heard the screams of billions of damned people in this hell.
And then he met Jesus, who told him to tell other people that hell was real.
Wiese states that his first experience ended with him (apparently after his resurrection) lying on the floor of his living room, screaming in terror.
For the 28 years of his life preceding that unforgettable night, Bill Wiese was a Christian believing what was written in the 'good news' about man's fate after his death.
It has to be admitted that the knowledge revealed there about the fate of the dead is capable of terrifying the most perverse horror writers and is unlikely to be preached to children in Sunday schools.

Here is this knowledge:

And I say unto you, Every one that is angry with his brother shall be liable to judgment. And whosoever shall say to his brother: Raka, he shall be subject to the High Council. And whosoever shall say to him: "Ungodly", shall be subject to the punishment of hell by fire. Mt. 5:22

The Son of man shall send forth his angels: these shall gather out of his kingdom all the reprobates, and them that commit iniquity, and shall cast

them into a fiery furnace: there shall be weeping and gnashing of teeth. Mt. 13. 41.42
So shall it be at the end of the world: the angels shall come forth, and shall exclude the wicked from among the righteous, and shall cast them into a fiery furnace; there shall be weeping and gnashing of teeth. Mt. 13 49.50

Then he will say to those on his left also: "Go away from me, you cursed, into everlasting fire, prepared for the devil and his angels! Mt. 25.41

„in flaming fire, inflicting punishment on those who do not acknowledge God and do not obey the Gospel of our Lord Jesus. As punishment they will suffer eternal destruction from the face of the Lord and from His mighty majesty".
2 Thessalonians 1:8,9

This also shall drink of the wine of the inflammation of God prepared, undiluted, in the cup of His wrath; and shall be tormented with fire and brimstone before the holy angels and before the Lamb. And the smoke of their torment ascendeth for ever and ever, and there is no rest day or night for the worshippers of the Beast and his image, and he who takes the mark of her name.   Revelation 14:10.11

And Death and Abyss were cast into the lake of fire. This is the second death - the lake of fire.
If anyone was not found written in the book of life, was cast into the lake of fire. Rev. 20:14.15

And for cowards, unbelievers, abominations, murderers, debauchees, guile-mongers, idolaters and all liars: A share in the lake burning with fire and brimstone. This is the second death. Rev 21:8

If therefore your right eye is a cause of sin to you, pluck it out and cast it away from you. For it is better for you that one of your members should perish, than that your whole body should be cast into hell. Mt. 5:29

Bill Wise, because of his belief in the above words of the Prince of Peace and his followers, that November night lay on the floor of his living room, screaming in terror. Bill built his belief in the existence of hell on his reading of the gospels. But where the founders of Christianity got their knowledge of the fate of the dead is not very clear, because a reading of the Jewish scriptures, which are part of the Old Testament and on the basis of which Christians created their religion, seems to contradict Christian wet fantasies about hell.

The word hell does not occur in the Old Testament. The word for the abode of the dead or their state is Sheol. Here is what the Old Testament teaches about the state of the dead:

„Do not put your trust in princes
Nor in a man in whom there is no deliverance.
When the breath leaves him, he returns to his ground, then his intentions are lost". Ps 146. 3.4

„Because the living know that they will die, and the dead know nothing at all, neither do they have any more payment, for their memory is forgotten. So is their love, as well as their hatred, as well as their jealousy - have long since faded away, and they no longer have any part in everything that happens under the sun.
...Every work that your hand encounters, undertake according to your strength! For there is no activity nor understanding, nor knowledge, nor wisdom in Sheol, to which you are going".
Sermon. 5.6.10

„And Jacob tore his garments, and girded his loins with sackcloth, and mourned for his son for a long time. And when all his sons and daughters sought to comfort him, he would not listen to comfort, saying, Already in sorrow will I descend after my son into Sheol. And his father [continued] to mourn for him". Genesis 37. 34.35

„It is not the dead who praise the Lord, none of those who descend into Sheol". Ps 115. 17

Sheol does not mean some hell where unbelievers will be tormented in fire for eternity, Sheol is death and the grave: "for there is no activity nor understanding, neither knowledge nor wisdom in Sheol, to which you are going', 'the dead know nothing at all'.
Christians invented hell to frighten unbelievers with it and to terrorise unbelievers in their own

ranks. Christians attributed all their own worst qualities and murderous instincts, evidenced by these immoral fantasies about hell, to Satan. The Old Testament states explicitly that it is not Satan at all who is responsible for the evil that has gone out into the world:

"I form the light, and create darkness: I make peace, and create evil: I the LORD do all these things" Isaiah 45.7

Christian claims about Satan and hell are mere invention. Christians, moreover, along with their founder Jesus, have missed the truth on more than just this occasion. Jesus prophesied thus about his second coming (another Christian invention, there is not even a word in the Old Testament about the second coming of the messiah):

„Verily I say unto you, Some of them that stand here shall not taste death, until they see the Son of man coming in his kingdom". Mt 16. 28

„In those days, after the tribulation, the sun will be eclipsed and the moon will not give its shine. The stars will fall from heaven and the powers in the sky will be shaken. Then they will see the Son of Man coming in the clouds with great power and glory. Then He will send angels and gather His elect from the four corners of the world, from the ends of the earth to the top of heaven...Truly, I say to you, this generation will not pass away

until all these things have happened. Heaven and earth will pass away, but my words will not pass away". Mk 13. 24-31

Following the example of Jesus, another prophet, Saul, made this prophecy some 2,000 years ago:

„Behold, I announce to you a mystery: we shall not all die, but we shall all be changed. In a moment, in the twinkling of an eye, at the sound of the last trumpet - for the trumpet will sound - the dead will rise unharmed, and we will be changed". 1 Cor. 15:51-52

These are further Christian lies for which, according to Jewish law, the false prophet who utters them should suffer death:

„I will raise up unto them a prophet from among their brethren, such as thou art, and will put my words in his mouth; he shall speak unto them all that I command. If any man will not listen to my words which he shall speak in my name, I will require of him an account. But if any prophet dares to speak in my name what I have not commanded him, or speaks in the name of foreign gods - such a prophet must suffer death.
If you think in your heart, "And how shall I know the word which the Lord has not spoken?" - when a prophet prophesies something in the name of the Lord, and his word will be without effect and will not be fulfilled, [it means that] this the Lord did not speak to him, but in his pride the prophet

himself said it. Thou shalt not be afraid of him".
Deuteronomy. 18. 18-22

On the basis of the Judeo-Christian Bible, therefore, it can be proven that Christians made up and lied from the beginning. The Jesus view of Satan should therefore be taken with great scepticism:

„You have the devil for a father and want to fulfil your father's desires. From the beginning he was a murderer and in the truth he did not persevere, because the truth is not in him. When he speaks a lie, from himself he speaks, for he is a liar and the father of lies. And because I speak the truth, therefore do you not believe Me. Who among you will prove Me a sin? If I speak the truth, why do you not believe Me? John 8: 44-46

"When he speaks a lie, from himself he speaks, for he is a liar and the father of lies."

Except that it is not Satan who has just been proven to be a liar.
Hell really exists. It is a reality in the heads of those who believe in it. Hell exists in the heads of people who believe in Jesus and his apostles, such as Bill Wiese, who, under the influence of the "truth of the gospel" on 22 lit November 1998, lay on the floor of his living room, screaming in terror.

Life After Death

The Christian Original Lie

"Behold, I announce to you a mystery: we shall not all die, but we shall all be changed. In one moment, in the twinkling of an eye, at the sound of the last trumpet - for the trumpet will sound - the dead will rise intact, and we will be changed. It is necessary that what is destructible should be clothed with indestructibility, and what is mortal should be clothed with immortality."   1 Corinthians 15: 51-53

This lie was told by one of the greatest Christian prophets, the Apostle Paul of Tarsus. "We shall

not all die..." said the prophet some 2,000 years ago. This passing proper of Christians was initiated by their founder, Jesus called by them the Christ:

"For the Son of Man shall come in the glory of his Father with his angels, and then he shall render to every one according to his conduct. Verily I say unto you, Some of them that stand here shall not taste death, until they see the Son of man coming in his kingdom."   Mt 16: 27.28

In case anyone dares to question the truths of the faith, the prophet Paul delivered another prophecy:

"...who go to perdition because they have not accepted the love of the truth (We shall not all die...) in order to obtain salvation. Therefore God permits deception to work on them, so that they will believe a lie, so that all who have not believed the truth (We shall not all die...) but have taken a liking to iniquity will be judged."
2 Thessalonians 2: 10-12

That is, blind faith is truth and the ability to reason logically is a lie and deception allowed by god. However, some people base their belief in life after death not only on religious scriptures, but also on a phenomenon called near-death experience (NDE).

Quoting from wikipedia: 'Neuroscientific research hypothesises that the NDE is a subjective phenomenon resulting from "disturbed bodily multisensory integration" that occurs during life-threatening events. Some transcendental and religious beliefs about the afterlife contain descriptions similar to NDEs. They describe sensations such as out-of-body experiences, a 'panoramic view of life', a light, a tunnel or a boundary.

Recently, quite by accident, scientists have made a fascinating study related to human death.

In a study published in Frontiers in Aging Neuroscience doctors took brain scans of a patient who had died during a test that detects electrical activity in the brain, called an electroencephalogram (EEG).

As the patient died during the test, the doctors gained an insight into the man's brain activity while dying. Such scans had never before been captured on a dying person. For about 30 seconds before and after the man's heart stopped beating, the scans showed increased activity in parts of the brain associated with memory recall, meditation and sleep.

"By generating oscillations involved in memory retrieval, the brain may play a last recall of important life events just before we die, similar to those reported in near-death experiences," said Ajmal Zemmar, a neurosurgeon at the University of Louisville in Kentucky.

In 2013, a similar study was conducted on rats. They too showed very similar brain activity just before and just after death in these animals.

Anyone who, like myself recently, has lost someone close to them knows the powerful emotions that accompany this. The sadness is overwhelming, the desire for one more conversation, one more look, the disbelief that the parting is final, that there is nothing there...

Religions prey precisely on these emotions, on this sadness and sense of loss, coming out with their offer of an imaginary life after life. It has been a lie from the beginning. However, I hope that the last visions of my loved one gave her eternal peace, and that the memories were only among the good ones. Because I know that life in flesh and blood was difficult. For some reason the followers of an imaginary god threaten me with annihilation in the fire, attribute iniquity, say my father is Satan because I sincerely hate their lie, but as I wrote in The Satanic Kerygma: "

„countless graves completely contradict the lie of eternal life".

Assisted Dying

Right to Death

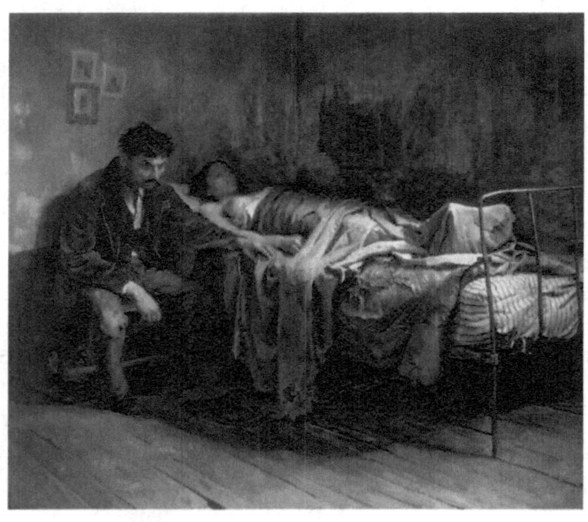

The Misery 1886-Painted by Cristóbal Rojas

Every living being has the right to life. A human being has a right to life, but no obligation to live. Every human being has come into existence as a result of the immutable laws of nature and can only function in accordance with those laws. Natural birth and the resulting inevitable and natural death are in accordance with the eternal laws of nature. As a result of the natural and as old as life itself law of inheritance, genetic mutations sometimes occur, as a result of which

genetic defects can occur in living beings, leading to disability, disease and death. These factors can cause immense physical and psychological suffering.

Human beings have a right to life and a right to death. The delusional Bronze Age desert god has no power over human life. His imaginary and incomprehensible plan for every human being does not exist. Human life depends on the eternal laws of nature.

A human being with an incurable disease (e.g. terminal cancer or neurodegenerative diseases), incurable pain or an associated unwillingness to continue living should have the option of assisted dying or refusal of life-prolonging treatment.

Faced with impending and unavoidable death, sick people should be able to opt for assisted dying as a medical option to shorten the dying process, which they perceive as unbearable.

Every human being should have the right to die with dignity.

Every human being should be provided with assistance in dying if necessary, which includes both euthanasia and physician-assisted suicide.

According to the definition, euthanasia is the knowing and intentional commission of an act with the express intention of ending the life of another person. Euthanasia is involved if:

the person suffers from a terminal illness; the person assisting knows of the person's condition; the person commits the act with the primary intention of ending the person's life; and the act is undertaken without personal gain.

Assisted dying means knowingly and intentionally providing a person with the knowledge or means required to commit suicide, including advising on lethal doses of medication, prescribing such lethal doses or providing medication.

As an example of a voluntary assisted dying procedure, let us refer to the law of the Australian state of Victoria posted on the Department of Health website.

Voluntary assisted dying - explanation

Voluntary assisted dying means that a person in the late stages of an advanced illness can take a substance prescribed by a doctor that will cause their death at a time of their choosing.

Only people who meet all the conditions and follow the procedure can access the voluntary assisted dying substance. A person's decision to request voluntary assisted dying must be voluntary (the person's decision)

permanent (the person makes three separate requests for voluntary assisted dying during the process)

fully informed (the person is well informed about their illness and the options for treatment and palliative care).

Conditions for access to voluntary assisted dying: People can request voluntary assisted dying if they meet all of the following conditions: They must have an advanced disease that will cause their death and which:

is likely to cause their death within six months (or within 12 months in the case of neurodegenerative diseases such as motor neurone disease)
causes suffering that the person is unable to accept.
The person must be able to make and communicate a decision about voluntary assisted dying during the formal application process.
They must also be an adult aged 18 years or older.
In addition to the form of euthanasia discussed above, there is also what is known as passive euthanasia.
The concept of passive euthanasia occurs when: A person voluntarily refuses food and liquids, this is also called voluntary cessation of food and drink, or when there is a refusal to feed and hydrate the patient.
If every human being has a right to life, then he or she must also have a right to death. A sane human being must have the right to decide on his or her life and death.
Life and death are processes in accordance with the natural law of nature. There cannot be a law that prohibits death and at the same time orders man to suffer unnecessary agony before its inevitable arrival.
And although this law is generally opposed by followers of delusional religions, even among them a voice of reason can be heard. This is how former Archbishop of Canterbury George Carey, who changed his mind on the subject after seeing cases of real suffering, commented on assisted

death: "The old philosophical certainties have collapsed in the face of the reality of unnecessary suffering. (...) By strictly adhering to the accepted teaching on the sanctity of life, the Church can actually sanction anguish and pain - the very opposite of the Christian message."

Not only can the Church sanction anguish and pain, but in its history it has proven itself to be a master of hypocrisy, proclaiming on the one hand the so-called sanctity of human life from the moment of conception until natural death, while at the same time it has specialised in inflicting anguish and pain and death on a mass scale, at which it has over time achieved perfection.

Satanism accepts an eternal, natural order of things that has existed since the beginning of reality, which may have no beginning or end. Satanism proclaims that a human being in his or her right mind has the right to decide his or her own destiny and that he or she will absolutely suffer the consequences of his or her choices. Satanism preaches that the right to die, like the right to live, is a human right. Satanism preaches that suffering is evil. A law that forces suffering is evil. A religion that preaches the virtue of suffering is an inhuman evil. Only a system based on the natural order of things can be perfect, just as the eternal, godless and indifferent universe is perfect.

On the Morality of Murder

Hey atheists, answer the question, is murder good or not? Give me the short answer, yes or no. Well, because how would we know if something is good or bad, moral or immoral if the bible didn't teach about it? Checkmate atheists.

Every now and then I come across such, or similar, displays of mental rectitude by adherents of Judeo-Christian theism on the internet. Given the fact that these queries or memes containing them are very similar to each other I assume that they come from some pseudo-intellectual theistic source, then are unreflectively copied and spread on the internet by people who have a huge problem with independent thinking and therefore rely entirely on the opinion of a so-called spiritual authority or other guru to come up with this kind of idiocy.

Before the above question can be answered in any way, the concept of murder must first be defined.

Murder according to the UN definition is: 'the unlawful deprivation of human life, with intent to cause death, or grievous bodily harm'. Law, as defined by Geoffrey Robertson, is a set of rules that are created and enforced by social or governmental institutions (and therefore by people) to regulate behaviour. Murder is therefore an act committed against an accepted set of rules.

It is worth adding that statistically, according to Donald Black, 90% of murders are revenge killings - retribution for acts previously committed by the victim against the perpetrator or his relatives. It seems to me that this statistic is quite relevant in determining the so-called morality of murder.

So is murder only proper for humans, and is it right or wrong because it is written in the Bible?

Scientists prove that herd animals are among the most intelligent animals. This is because the group teaches cooperation and collaboration to benefit the group, which translates into greater benefits for the individual member of the group, and an increased chance of survival for the individual thanks to the group.

Ants, bees, termites, wolves, lycas, buffaloes, elephants, chimpanzees, or hyenas, and human animals have proved over the centuries that it is possible to succeed in the age-old struggle for survival by working together as a group.

Ants or bees have created their communities divided into classes. Their groups have slaves, workers, warriors and queens. When threatened, warriors throw themselves at the enemy without hesitation, very often giving their lives in the fight to defend their community. Bees, for example, have a very interesting defensive tactic that they use to defend themselves against their greatest enemies, the hornets. Hornets are the bees' mortal enemies. When they find a bee hive,

they can slaughter all the bees inside it in a very short time. So the bees, when they discover a hornet that has got into their hive, immediately surround it tightly on all sides and start flapping their wings, thus generating such a high temperature that the hornet is boiled alive in it. Bees which have taken part in this defensive mission also lose their lives in the process. So the bees carry out a murder on the hornet, defending their community, sacrificing their own lives in the process. Do bees read the Bible? How do they know if they are doing the morally right thing? Why do they sacrifice themselves?

Among vertebrates, interesting forms of behaviour have been observed in Hyenas. Hyenas form very tightly-knit groups, forming family communities. The hyena group is always led by a dominant female. Thanks to their excellent cooperation and understanding of their place in the group hierarchy, hyenas are excellent hunters and are able to take even lions' prey in a coordinated manner. In one such group, researchers observed an interesting case of a power struggle. The group was led by a very strong female, who, however, became increasingly aggressive, cruel and selfish over time. She stopped paying attention to the other members of the herd and, when hunting, attacked other members of the herd and tried to seize the prey just for herself. At one point, the other hyenas, fed up with the dictatorship of the cruel leader, organised a mutiny, attacked the despot together, injured her very badly, threw

her out of the group and left her alone on the savannah to die. Was the hyenas' behaviour good or bad? How did the hyenas know what was good for the survival of the group?
I have only given two examples out of an infinite number of similar cases occurring in the animal world, of which man is also one.

Hundreds of thousands of years before the biblical Bronze Age, other hominin species walked the earth; australopithecines, homo erectus, or Neanderthals among others. They too formed communities, interacted as a group, hunted together and supported each other in order to survive. They followed rules that they themselves created in order for the group to succeed in the struggle for survival. Pathological individuals, as in the case of the hyenas above, were eliminated from the group because they threatened its survival, whereas killing for the good of the community was useful.
In Asia, long before the Bronze Age, there were societies that did not know the Bible, which created great civilisations (it is interesting that the authors of the Bible had no idea of the existence of people living in China or India).
Without the knowledge of the Bible, why didn't the people living there kill each other driven by godless selfishness?
In fact, in the times and places described in the Bible itself, apart from a group of Jews in the desert, there were other communities and even powerful states which made their own laws in

order to serve the community and within which the community could develop and cooperate without threatening its own existence. The Jews, like all other communities, simply created their own set of laws and rules of group conduct to serve their survival and function. Many of these laws, by the way, were taken by the biblical writers from pre-existing codes, such as the Babylonian Code of Hammurabi. These communities created sets of laws and rules of conduct that they believed would benefit the group. Crimes committed against the set of rules established in a community were severely punished because such acts were harmful to the group.

So is murder good or bad? In my opinion, the correct question should be: is murder useful at the time or not? If the murder is committed for the benefit of the community, then the act becomes morally justifiable for the community. Therefore, the notion of some objective morality is a purely abstract concept. The theistic, speculative way of thinking is for the most part completely abstract. In practice, a given concept acquires its true meaning when applied to a concrete, real-life case, and then these abstract concepts make sense, or not. If they are devoid of practical meaning then they should be abandoned. To pretend that some system based on purely speculative and abstract concepts is reality is a mistake and a lie. On the other hand, a system of concepts that grows out of an observable godless reality, verifiable in a concrete,

real-life situation, and whose practicality of concepts can be proven is true, because, as we know, the devil is in the details.

The next chapters of the book will again be devoted to the Godless Theology of Ecclesia Luciferi and an introduction to satanic magic according to the Ecclesia Luciferi system.

Impietas - God's fear

The Expulsion from Paradise - Albrecht Dürer

Here is the unrevealed truth: God cannot be killed by any weapon, god can only be killed by a lack of faith in him. It is godlessness that is the true power of the god-killer.

The Christian messiah Jesus and his disciples seem to have been well aware of this.

Nowhere in their Bible did the Christians portray the followers of a personal Satan, or in common understanding, believers in a personal Satan, as their main opponents. Moreover, they knew of no self-proclaimed followers of Satan. But what they niustically stigmatised was unbelief.

Christians threatened all ungodly people, i.e. those who did not believe in God, in Jesus and in his teachings, with death in hellfire in the end.

„But as for cowards, unbelievers, the degraded, murderers, the impure, sorcerers, idolaters, and all liars--their place will be in the burning lake of fire and sulphur. That is the Second Death."
Rev 21:8
"... also the cities of Sodom and Gomorrah, having turned them to ashes, he condemned to destruction, setting an example [of punishment] to those who would live ungodly" 2 Peter 2:6

"... who go to perdition because they have not accepted the love of the truth (gospel) in order to receive salvation. Therefore God permits deception to come upon them, that they may believe a lie, so that all who have not believed the truth (the gospel) but have taken pleasure in iniquity will be judged." 2 Thess. 2:10-12

These threats overlap with those in the Old Testament:

„The sinners in Zion are terrified; trembling grips the godless: "Who among us can live with the consuming fire? Who among us can live with everlasting flames?" Isa 33:14

In keeping with this spirit of original Christian love, one of the followers of Jesus called the "Apostle of the nations" in his letters heaps the severest epithets on unbelievers:

"For the wrath of God is revealed from heaven upon all ungodliness and unrighteousness of those people who by unrighteousness impose restraints upon the truth...Therefore God has given them over to feckless passions: namely, their women have changed a life according to nature into one contrary to nature. Likewise, men, having abandoned normal cohabitation with women, became inflamed with lust for one another, men with men practising shamelessness and bearing on themselves the wages due for perversion. And because they did not deem it right to retain the true knowledge of God (faith), God gave them over to an unfit mind, so that they did what was not fitting. They are also full of all kinds of iniquity, perversity, covetousness, wickedness. Devoted to envy, murder, feuds, deceit, malice; slanderers, slanderers, haters of God, insolent, proud, boastful, in what is evil ingenuous, disobedient to parents, without understanding, unsteady, heartless, without mercy. These, although they know well the judgment of God, that those who commit such deeds are guilty of death, not only commit them, but moreover glorify those who do them." Rom 1:18-32

Not only does Jesus' ablest propagandist call out unbelievers using every insult known to him, but on top of that, he claims that they use an unfit mind for nothing.
The apostle of blind faith, in another epistle, calls knowledge false in contrast to faith and orders to avoid debating ideas contrary to faith:

„O Timothy, guard and keep safe the deposit [of godly truth] entrusted to you, turn away from worldly and godless chatter [with its profane, empty words], and the contradictions of what is falsely called "knowledge""   *1 Timothy 6:20*

And Jesus does not even hesitate to call his disciple Peter, an unbeliever in his words, Satan himself:

"Henceforth Jesus began to point out to His disciples that He must go up to Jerusalem and suffer much from the elders and chief priests and scribes; that He would be killed and rise from the dead on the third day. And Peter took Him aside and began to reproach Him: "Lord, may God protect you! This will never come upon you." But He turned and said to Peter: "Get out of My sight, Satan! You are a stumbling block to Me, because you think not in God's way but in man's way".
Mt 16:21-23

An examination of the New Testament writings shows that Christian theology does not pay any attention at all to worshippers of a personal devil.

Probably because devil worshippers also believe in a god. Their greatest enemy, on the other hand, is unbelief.

"And every spirit who does not recognise Jesus is not of God; and this is the spirit of Antichrist, who, as you have heard, is coming and is already in the world". 1 John 4:3

"Who is a liar, if not he who denies that Jesus is the Christ? He is the antichrist who casts doubt on the Father and the Son." 1 John 2:22

"For many deceivers have gone out into the world who refuse to acknowledge that Jesus Christ came in the flesh. Such a one is a deceiver and antichrist." 2 John 1:7

It is the spirit of Antichrist that is behind unbelief. It is godlessness that is satanic.
Godlessness, by all theistic religions, is seen as the greatest evil. The followers of these religions, out of fear of its power, do not even hesitate to commit acts of violence, along with the murder of non-believers in their delusions. Religion gives them truly narcotic raptures, and the priest-dealers jealously make sure that the faithful do not break free from this narcotic trance.
The Ecclesia Luciferi is an outgrowth of the spirit of the Antichrist, breaking the theistic, narcotic religious spell, a truly satanic system or path

binding to total godlessness, the only weapon with the power to kill the gods.

Descent Into Hell

I was dead, and behold, I am alive

Édouard Manet - Le Suicidé (1877)

The book **The Satanic Kerygma** is, for the most part, written in the form of a parable, and its teachings are allegorical, so I have decided to discuss here a certain passage of it which describes a very important issue, the meaning of which I would like to explain a little further.

The passage to which I wish to draw attention includes the subsections from: Dead in Satan to The Ascension. **The Satanic Kerygma vv. 454-462**

I would like to focus here particularly on the passage: Transition Phase - Descent into Hell.

Here are its contents:

Dead in Satan

The symbol of immersion in blood, signifies the descent into death of the spirit who dies with Lucifer for the sake of superstition because of the new life in flesh and blood: We die with him to rise to undead life in flesh and blood due to the glory of Satanic Self-consciousness.

Transition Phase - Descent into Hell

During the transformation of the death of the spirit, the consciousness can sometimes experience fear and confusion inherent in the emptiness of the land of the dead. Lucifer, however, descended there first to free its prisoners.
The land of the dead into which Lucifer descended is called Hell because those who find themselves there are deprived of the joy of an imaginary paradise, the presence of a deity and the false hope-giving belief in eternal life.
Such a state does not necessarily apply to everyone, but can be experienced by those most indoctrinated by religious superstition. Lucifer's descent into hell, however, slowly releases Satanic self-consciousness in all who end up there, in consequence of which those who truly desire it will return from the hell of heavenly illusions to a life abundant in flesh and blood. Lucifer did not descend into hell to liberate the blind who do not

wish to see, nor to destroy their hell , but to restore the spiritual living dead to bodily life .

The descent into hell is the consequence of the complete denial of the philosophy of delusional crime and the eternal punishment for it. It is the final phase of the rejection of the false message of the doctrine of eternal life as a reward for blind faith, a phase rather short-lived but of immense power in its mysterious sense of spreading godlessness to all who desire the death of the delusion, so that all those who are damned become the liberators of Hell.

Lucifer descended into Hell so that those who died to superstition would hear the whisper of Satan's being, and, following it, rise to a life abundant in flesh and blood. The Light-Bearer, by the power of knowledge, has defeated him who held the power of delusional eternal life, that is, god, and has liberated all those who all their lives through fear of death and punishment after death were subject to the bondage of superstition. Lucifer has the seal of Death and Hell".

The above passage deals with the transformation that a person can experience when trying to free himself from the hell of theistic delusions and the way - the stages - of his ungodly transformation, from death to life in religious delusions to resurrection to the one sure, abundant life in the glory of flesh and blood.

This path and this kind of transformation does not apply to everyone, but there are those, and I know there are a legion of them, who recognise their struggle in it. Let their power and symbol

for liberation be Lucifer, who fearlessly and regretlessly rejected belief in a false god and in an imaginary eternal life, who became the first sinner, the first cursed, and whose curse was inherited by the whole natural order of things; the only true one that exists for sure.
The above excerpt from The Satanic Kerygma is related to an issue known as Religious trauma syndrome (RTS).
In an article entitled Thou Shalt Not: Treating Religious Trauma and Spiritual Harm With Combined Therapy author Alyson M. Stone describes RTS as 'the severe psychological distress experienced by former fundamentalist Christians who leave their religion'. The author defines the term as psychological damage caused by religious belief and experiences.
Symptoms of RTS include fear and guilt:

"...religious systems that use fear of God and hell and social ostracism to motivate and control become psychologically toxic and violent".
"Although many people may feel guilty when experiencing negative emotions, religion-based fear can intensify the experience of 'I am a bad person because I feel so despicable' into 'I am a blameworthy person for feeling so inferior".

Psychologists believe that RTS symptoms are a natural reaction to the perceived existence of a brutal, all-powerful God who sees people as inherently flawed, along with regular exposure to religious leaders who use the threat of eternal

death, unredeemable life, demon possession and many other frightening ideas to control the religious devotion and submission of group members.

Religious trauma syndrome is the consequence of the mind being infected by the virus of theistic religion. The disease develops and progresses slowly and may not be noticeable at first. According to psychologists, unlike many forms of trauma that occur as a result of acute incidents, religious trauma generally builds up gradually through prolonged exposure to messages that undermine mental health. Many people are born into belief systems in their families and religious communities, and it is in these early groups that they are immersed in messages that influence their ideas about themselves and the world.

Healing from the disease of theism and killing the virus of religion can be a long and painful process for some, as can healing from a serious, life-threatening illness, but it is nevertheless as possible and necessary to achieve a truly abundant life of godlessness. The Satanic Kerygma is designed to sow Luciferian doubt of an imaginary paradise in the minds of followers of false deities, scepticism leading to acceptance of the gift of a true, delusion-free life in the glory of flesh and blood, in the glory of natural sinfulness.

The Satanic Kerygma recognises and sees the true essence of the danger that theism presents.

The mystery of godlessness is the antidote to the yahwistic poison.

Satanic Magic

To make yourself invisible

Acquire seven black beans. Start the whole rite on Wednesday, before sunrise. Take the head of a dead man and place one bean in its mouth, two in the cavity of the nose, two in the eye sockets, two in the ears, on the head make the character you find in the engraving. And when you have done everything bury the head so that the face faces upwards. For nine days, before sunrise, water it every morning using the best brandy. On the eighth day you will find the said spirit asking you the question, "What is withering here?" You, in turn, will answer: "I am watering my plant." Then the spirit will say: "Give me the bottle, I wish to water it myself." In response you must refuse him, even if he repeats the request. Then he will extend his hand and show you the same figure you have drawn on your head. Then you can be sure that you are dealing with the right spirit, the spirit of the head. This is because there is a danger that some other spirit might try to deceive you, which would have bad consequences, in which case your operation would certainly fail. Only then can you give him the bottle, and he will water his head and leave. The next day, which is the ninth, when you return, you will see that the beans have germinated. Take the sprout and place it in your mouth and look at your reflection in the mirror, if you don't see anything it is good, in the same way you can try the others, you can

place them either in your mouth or in the child's mouth. Those seeds that don't produce the invisibility effect should be buried with your head.

How to make a girl dance naked

Write on virgin parchment the first character from the figure shown here, do it with the blood of a bat. Later, place it on the blessed stone over which the Mass was recited. After this, whenever you wish to use it, place it under the threshold, or under the door through which she will have to pass. And when she passes through, then she will go into a strange frenzy, she will undress and become completely naked. And when she begins to dance, if no one pulls this sign, she will dance until she dies, her face will be twisted and her body will twist, arousing more compassion and pity than desire.

The grotesque magical rituals presented above are taken from the work entitled: **"Grimorium Verum"**, supposedly written in 1517, but actually written most likely in the mid-18th century.

What is magic?

Magic can be defined as a body of beliefs and practices based on the belief in the existence of supernatural forces that can be controlled by means of appropriate spells and specific actions.

The above rituals are an example of how ridiculous, grotesque and idiotic a belief in supernatural reality and supernatural powers can take form.

However, I do not deny that there is 'magic' which holds that the subconscious is responsible for magical actions and can be programmed to achieve the desired changes. This programming takes place through the use of symbols and autosuggestion in a state of mind which, for example, Buddhists call samadhi and the chaots call gnosis.

Christians, such as Pentecostals, for example, can, with the right techniques and a strong belief in supernatural reality, put themselves into a state resembling collective hysteria, during which they may mumble something in unintelligible languages or even experience hallucinations.

If hallucinations, hysteria, fainting spells and meaningless babbling are to be called magic, then such 'magic' does indeed exist. Nevertheless, the human mind, still mysterious, with its subconscious, with its not fully understood phenomenon of self-awareness, can hide whole magical worlds, sometimes manifested in dark dreams. It is there that still undiscovered and unrecognised, dark, fiendishly beautiful and blasphemous powers are hidden.

They may become accessible to some people determined enough to dare to look there.

And here I would like to present some „magical" practices of the Ecclesia Luciferi system. These

techniques can produce various phenomena and visions in persistent adepts.

The following chapter is closely linked to the book **Extrema Unctio. Satanic Last Rites** and can be fully understood after reading this book.

The Magus of Ecclesia Luciferi

The Magician (I), from the Rider-Waite tarot deck

In the main text of the book Extrema Unctio, which contains the satanic rite of passage - Path Towards Voidness, it is written that sometimes some adepts may have difficulty in understanding the essence of the phenomena they experience when they feel very strong emotions accompanying the unusual state they are in, and that this may be due to their unfamiliarity with magical practices (meditation and visualisation) because they have not engaged in such practices during their lifetime. In this

connection, I would like to give an example of some techniques that can be practised and which may be helpful in understanding the phenomena that appear before death.

First, however, I will present the nature of these phenomena from a more scientific point of view. **Iona Miller**, in her article **How the Brain Creates God**, writes on the subject as follows:

"When the senses and mind cease to function actively, the body becomes like a corpse. The death of the ego mirrors the process of a near-death experience (NDE)."

"Our response to religious words is mediated at the junction of the three lobes (parietal, frontal and temporal) and regulates the response to language. "The 'voice of God' probably emanates from electrical activity in the temporal lobes, which are important for speech perception. Internal speech is interpreted as coming from outside ourselves when Broca's area is switched on.

Stress can affect our ability to determine the origin of the voice. It is part of our fight or flight response, which can mobilise even when we are trying to relax. Non-stressful phenomena can include panic reactions, waving sighs, excessive heat, chills and skin trembling, throat constriction, watery eyes, flashes of light or waves in front of the eyes, sudden muscle spasms, tingling sensations and electric shock.

The right frontal cingulate cortex changes depending on whether the stimulus comes from

the environment or is an auditory hallucination. A wide range of mystical sounds have been described, from the buzzing of bees, to the sounds of bells, stringed instruments, thunder, distant echoes, ocean waves, wind and muffled conversations in unknown languages.

The ability to construct internal representations of sensory stimuli lies at the heart of perception and cognition. Viewed objectively, these mindscapes are perfectly concrete manifestations, but they also have a subjective aspect when we become aware of them. Our consciousness is experienced through our perception.

Each individual perception of the universe can occur as an internal or external experience. We can experience various forms of I-Thou dialogue along a continuum of extreme hyper- or hypo-awakening. Sacred images are generated in the inferior temporal lobe, which also responds to the ritual use of images and iconography. Empathy needs a face. Fear and incredulity arise in the amygdala body. Religious emotions arise in the middle temporal lobe, generating bliss, awe, joy and other feelings of well-being, as well as a sense of Presence."

After this more scientific introduction, we can now turn to the esoteric dimension of these phenomena. These phenomena and the techniques presented here have been known for hundreds of years. Their effectiveness has been proven. It is only the terminology,

the nomenclature and the approach to certain issues that are slightly different.
I emphasise that this is only an outline of the subject.
First an excerpted from the book **The Satanic Kerygma**:

The Visible and the Invisible

Images of Demons

Reality of Demons - Extra-corporeal Reality
„Immaterial, non-corporeal beings are real like dreams. They belong to the domain of the inner worlds.

Who are the images of demons?

Demons are creations of Satanic Self-consciousness.
By what appearances they make they may be called spirits, but in view of their task they are demons. Demons are servants and emissaries of Satanic Being.
Because always subordinated to the purpose of deception, they are the executors of His orders.
Demons, beings from the inner darkness, can take over the reason and will of those who are weak or untrained in controlling them: they can become as present as if they were real. As a result of the error or recklessness of the visualiser, they can, with their sinful perfection, rise above human will and reason. They have the power to compel

the performance of dark and terrible things. Including ultimate things.
Lucifer is the centre of the inner demonic circle. Images of demons belong to Him, because He has the greatest power to compel the subconscious to create any sinful entity.
Even more so, they belong to Him because He has made them emissaries of His plan of deception to those who call upon them.
The images of the demons are present from the moment they are projected and throughout the hallucination".

This text is primarily concerned with one way of achieving a state of Satanic Self-Awareness. This is a state similar to that known, for example, in Esoteric Buddhism as Luminosity. This state can be achieved through various practices and techniques. One such method is to consciously enter a state of deep dreaming, and if the practitioner is able to remain conscious during this deep dreaming, he or she will be able to recognise the so-called luminosity of death and ultimately achieve the state of the Enlightened One.

In order to induce conscious dreaming, researchers such as Laberge and Kelzer, and others have attempted to develop methods of inducing it. Steven Laberge, for example, developed a technique called mnemonic induction of conscious dreams (MILD) which involves waking up at night after a dream,

focusing mainly on the dream's incongruities, and deciding that if any incongruity of the dream reappears, it will immediately become conscious. Laberge has even developed special dreamlight goggles that flash a low-intensity light with the occurrence of rapid eye movements during the R.E.M sleep phase that characterise the onset of dreaming.

Other techniques propose entering conscious dreaming by focusing on naturally occurring hypnogogic images (a type of hallucination, i.e. confusing visual, auditory, olfactory or tactile sensory perceptions that appear authentic, although they occur without sensory input) that occur prior to the onset of dreaming, and the autosuggestion that the dreamer will immediately become conscious after recognising inconsistencies in the dream state. (For example, realising that the observed scene is inconsistent with the laws of physics). Awareness of this inconsistency triggered a conscious dream. Further techniques use autosuggestion, the determination that a person will be conscious in their dreams.

Hallucinogenic plants such as Bard's Sage or meditation recordings or recordings of so-called binural sounds are also used in achieving a conscious dream state. However, special meditation methods such as sleep yoga are most recommended.

In a study published by Julian Mutz and Amir-Homayoun Javadi in Neuroscience of Consciousness in 2017, the authors showed that

people who practise meditation for longer periods of time have a higher number of conscious dreams.

Within the tantric system, the specific practice of dream yoga is oriented towards preparing the practitioner for the after-death state which is exactly the topic of interest in this book.
This is how Namkhai Norbu writes on the subject:

"There is a correspondence between dreaming and dreaming states and our experiences when we die. When one dies, first of all the senses disappear . ...We are talking about the moment when the senses disappear within us...At this point, the person experiences many sensations of the disappearance or withdrawal of the senses. Then comes a state similar to unconsciousness; it is similar to fainting. Then begins what is called the emergence of the four lights (seeing the lights).
The truth is that it is as if you have fainted and - with the appearance of the lights - slowly, slowly consciousness begins to awaken."

So the most desirable i.e. meditative technique for inducing a conscious satanic dream might look like the following:
Before going to sleep, visualise and concentrate on the figure of Baphomet (or another deity) at the centre of your body. The image of Baphomet should appear together with the sound of Uss, resembling the hissing of a snake.

You may find it helpful to use a picture with Baphomet's likeness in the visualisation; place the picture in front of you and stare at it for a moment. Close your eyes and Baphomet will immediately appear in front of your mind. Concentrate on him and stay with him for as long as you can. The most important thing is to keep Baphomet present with you as you fall asleep.

You maintain the presence of this visualisation, relax and slowly, slowly fall asleep. If one learns to fall asleep in this way, he finds the full presence of the luciferic light state. He then falls asleep and sleeps almost consciously. He is then able to recognise that he is dreaming.

However, such concentration may initially be difficult.

Locking oneself in a dark room for three days can then be helpful in maximising concentration. At this point, it should be emphasised that the conscious dreaming techniques presented here are not for everyone. A practitioner of these techniques over a prolonged period of time may experience a confusion of dreams and reality, he or she may also experience conscious dreaming during a nightmare. It is therefore very important to learn to recognise the signs of dreaming and to learn to distinguish between them.

These techniques are not for mentally unstable people. Satanism is not for mentally unstable or weak people.

Consciousness during sleep allows the satanist to develop. In this state, it is possible to manipulate

the dream and therefore the emerging reality. It is then possible to travel to any place, even to a lost paradise. It is possible to transform people into beasts or if one wants to dream of Lucifer one should think of transforming oneself into him by concentrating completely on him.

An interesting and helpful technique is to imagine during the day that one is living a dream, then at night the dream itself will also seem no less real.

One should learn to spontaneously visualise Baphomet, without thinking or creating, and then relax and fall asleep. You can place his image next to or above your bed. When you wake up in the morning you should immediately make a Uss hissing sound, loud enough to hear yourself and feel the presence of the deity.

Several of the techniques mentioned here are aimed at achieving a hybrid state of consciousness having the characteristics of both the real world and a dream, during which it would be advisable to try to transform this newly created reality.

Once a person has learned to experience such a state, he or she can begin to practice visualising themselves as a deity - Lucifer - the Luminosity. Transforming one's own identity into that of the divine.

By practising meditation on reality as dream-like, and the methods described above, such visualisation can be perceived as no less real than everyday reality.

This transformation of identity into a completely godless entity can also be seen as a kind of possession. Its course and effects are described in the book **The Satanic Kerygma** as follows:

With a kind of possession, man in unconsciousness turns to the Sinful Being as if to a dark god and communes with him in order to invite him into communion with himself and receive him into it. The response to this is the gift of doubt.
During doubt, man surrenders his reason and his will completely to the Being. With his whole corporeal being, man expresses the acquiescence of the Anti-God. The system of unbelief calls man's response to the Anti-God manifested in him a possession".

Because according to The Satanic Kerygma: "Lucifer is the centre of the inner demonic circle. The images of demons belong to him, because he has the greatest power to compel the subconscious to create every sinful entity". It is up to the practitioner to be able to create images of demons.
These demons are visualisations of emotions commonly considered 'negative'. According to a tantric practice called transformation theory, these 'negative' emotions such as lust, hatred, greed, pride are used as part of the path. As necessary elements on the path to true liberation. These things that people think are bad, visualised, serve my will. I control them and can transform

them at will. I will use them to achieve the goal, perfect indifference. True enlightenment involves transcending attachment to dual categories such as pure and impure, permitted and forbidden (good and bad).

As the Guhyasamaja Tantra states, 'the sage who makes no distinction attains the state of the Awakened One'.

If the practitioner has the will to attribute some demon names to these emotions or the signs corresponding to these demons called sigils, he can do so. At all times, however, he must remember that it is he, Lucifer, who has arisen from a transformed identity, who is their master.

Yet another very interesting technique for approaching the state of Satanic Self-Consciousness is one based on one of the Illusory Body/Luminosity practices. It involves the practitioner sitting down in front of a mirror and hanging an image representing for example Baphomet, Satan or a chosen demon behind him or her, so that his or her image appears in the mirror placed in front. The practitioner then stares at the image as his or her reflection (he or she can also talk to the image as his or her reflection) and checks if there is any emotional reaction.

Once any emotional reaction is gone, the practitioner should recognise the truth that everything is devoid of essence, as is the body of the deity.

This is about approaching a state of emptiness.
The state of emptiness and nothingness is the ultimate state.
Ultimately, however, the innate, luminous, Luciferian nature of the mind is experienced in the process of dying, when pure light appears.

The above practices bring the practitioner closer to experiencing this state while still in the one true life. For when the light disappears, the end comes.
The "rituals" presented here are techniques and methods drawn mostly from these practices of the centuries-old Eastern spiritual tradition, which are also often supported by the latest scientific research in the fields of neuroscience and consciousness. The states achieved through the application of these techniques are also achievable through scientific techniques. These methods help to experience the state of perfect indifference (of the universe) desired by Ecclesia Luciferi, which can be called inner peace.
The Luciferian luminosity to which we aspire can be achieved by various methods. The most important thing is that we attain it. Every theistic deity is its enemy because it leads to the truth of indistinguishability, beyond good and evil, to absolute godlessness and indifference.

Lucifer Arisen

Godless Satanism Doctrine

The Fallen Angel - Alexandre Cabanel 1847

"One hears without seeking, one takes without asking who gives; thought shoots out like lightning, with necessity, in form without hesitation - I never had a choice. Enchantment, the tension of which was sometimes released in a stream of tears ... a depth of happiness in which what is most painful and gloomiest does not act as a contradiction, but as something conditioned, evoked, as a necessary colour among such an excess of light" **Friedrich Nietzsche "Ecce Homo".**

According to the godless theology of the Satanic System Ecclesia Luciferi, a Luciferian is a being who, through the practice of recognising and accepting the morally indifferent and natural instincts of the human animal, magic (meditation (magical-meditative practices (see book Extrema Unctio) are supposed to reveal a state/lead to a state similar to, as it were, conscious dying and rebirth as Lucifer - the Light-bearer)) and the development of godless wisdom has seen the true Luciferian nature of things (indifference to the universe and the laws of nature, the absence of religious (a)morality, the natural godlessness of nature, the power of the instincts, the final and certain death of all life instead of speculation and delusions about the life of the soul after the death of the body), which reality is attributed by theistic theology to the fall of nature into sin stemming from rebellion against theistic dictatorship.

The ability to truly recognise spiritual phenomena, bodily phenomena and the nature of the pure luciferic mind (self-aware and self-illuminating) leads to awakening (the attainment of perfect enlightenment when the obscurations from unknowing - ignorance - are transcended), which frees one forever from the suffering of a circle of delusions, unfounded beliefs, irrational fear and equally irrational guilt.

A being who has awakened from the sleep of ignorance through the discovery of the true nature of reality is called a Light-Bearer. (see Biblia Satanae)

The Awakened/Light-Bearer is a being who shares the true sin nature with the entire perfectly indifferent universe. In reality, everyone is enlightened. However, not everyone has yet recognised and accepted their natural instincts, their true sinful nature.

Luciferian awakening is a holistic change of consciousness, whereby one ceases to see the world as something separate from the concept of the' self'. The human animal and fallen nature are one. The theistic illusion of human separation from nature and the false consciousness of existing outside or above the natural world is a delusion and a lie.

Luciferian enlightenment is achieved independently by insight into one's own perfectly sinful true nature and by reaching a state of inner understanding through insight into the true Luciferian (luminous) nature of the mind and then achieving permanent contact with it. The melding of the self with the fallen nature.

Achieving a state of indifference - emptyness of a perfectly godless universe

(a liberating understanding of the true nature of things - not to be confused with apathy, depression or dementing illness) and satanic indiscrimination.

It is a complete denial of theistic theology and the divine plan of salvation.

It is self-salvation. The blood sacrifice of a false messiah becomes unnecessary.

Ecclesia Luciferi's
more important books

Biblia Satanae

Biblia Satanae, not by an imaginary deity, but by Man, is inspired, useful for satanic teaching, for detecting theistic superstition, for educating in godlessness, for proclaiming the good news of Lightbearer who has revealed Himself to free from belief in an imaginary god, from fear of death and divine fire, from guilt for sin that never was, from belief in eternal life on one's knees. So that the Satanist would be perfect, for a life abundant in flesh and blood prepared

The Satanic Kerygma

The Satanic Kerygma is a satanic book that contains a godless theology - the mystery of godlessness. It constitutes a study of theistic delusional truths and the path of man's transformation to a state of total godlessness.

Missale Satanae

The satanic missal **"Missale Satanae"** contains a detailed description of the preparation and performance of the satanic rituals of the Black Mass and Satanic exorcism according to the impious rite of Ecclesia Luciferi System.

www.ingramcontent.com/pod-product-compliance
Lightning Source LLC
La Vergne TN
LVHW090000180726
843489LV00001B/309